Advance Praise for
The Whole Systems Approach

"*The Whole Systems Approach* is an invaluable resource for leaders undertaking a challenging transformation. It is extremely helpful in providing an overview of the many subtleties of organizational change."

—Mark S. Lerner, COO of GOJO Industries, Inc.

"I liked this book a lot! It clearly is about results and building organizations that can sustain high levels of value creation while addressing the most basic needs of people who work in organizations—to be heard, respected, and validated, and to be authentically a part of the journey."

—Cory Foster, Intermedia Communications, Inc.

"*The Whole Systems Approach* is the most comprehensive and inclusive look at the interdependence of leaders and employees in managing and sustaining organizational change. This is a must-read for any manager, HR professional, or employee who wants to be enlightened about the dynamics of the business world in which we live to better survive and thrive in it."

—Janice Gurny, Senior VP of Human Resources,
Merrill Lynch

"What seems like a radical alternative to reengineering is really a 'nuts-and-bolts' approach to building a process-driven, customer-focused, team-based organization. Better yet, the results from *The Whole Systems Approach* will be sustained long after the initial changes are in place. I highly recommend this book to anyone looking for a better way."

—Larry L. Payne, Senior VP of Operations,
Blue Cross/Blue Shield of Florida

"This book really represents a picture of our lives at FSITI and the story of how we developed our current culture of excellence. People who have not experienced the exhilaration of having everyone committed to achieve a common goal cannot fully appreciate the power of this possibility or of what can be accomplished when everyone understands and is aligned to where the organization is going."

—Al Pino, President of First Security Information Technology, Inc.

The Whole Systems Approach is a pragmatic instruction manual for organizational soaring! Bill and Cindy Adams have given organizational leaders a compelling vision, a clear implementation plan, and an array of original tools needed to change compliance into commitment and to transform adequate into awesome."

—Chip R. Bell, author of *Customers as Partners*, *Dance Lessons*, and *Beep! Beep!*

The WHOLE Systems

APPROACH

*Involving Everyone in the Company
to Transform and Run Your Business*

W. A. (Bill) Adams and Cindy Adams
with Michael Bowker

Executive Excellence Publishing
1344 East 1120 South
Provo, UT 84606
phone: (801) 375-4060
fax: (801) 377-5960
e-mail: books@eep.com
web: http://www.eep.com

Ordering Information:

Individual Sales: Executive Excellence Publishing products are available through most bookstores. They can also be ordered directly from Executive Excellence at the address above.

Quantity Sales: Executive Excellence Publishing products are available at special quantity discounts when purchased in bulk by corporations, associations, libraries, and others, or for college textbook/course adoptions. Please write to the address above or call Executive Excellence Publishing, Book Sales Division, at 1-800-304-9782.

Orders for U.S. and Canadian trade bookstores and wholesalers: Executive Excellence Publishing books and audiotapes are available to the trade through LPC Group/Login Trade. Please contact LPC at 1436 West Randolph Street, Chicago, IL 60607, or call 1-800-626-4330.

First edition

Printed in the United States of America

10 9 8 7 6 5 4 3 2 1   03 02 01 00 99

ISBN 1-890009-41-5

The Whole Systems Approach is a service mark of Maxcomm Associates, Inc.

Cover design by Ginger McGovern
Cover art by Spatafore and Associates
Author photos by Brent Henridge and Associates, and Joanne McCubrey
Printed by Publishers Press

Dedication

To Bob Solum—a person who lived fully, taught richly and loved genuinely. We began this book project with Robert "Bob" Solum, our friend, comrade and partner; however, Bob passed from this world before the project was completed.

We were not allowed to finish the book with him in the flesh; yet, at times, we did feel his presence and spirit and are grateful for having had the opportunity of crossing his path.

Bob's life was filled with many people who all felt they were his best friend. We were two of those people. We think of him often and dedicate this book to his memory.

Acknowledgments

We feel deeply indebted to those special people in our lives who have, in some way, played a significant role in our personal and professional development and the evolution of our ideas. Therefore, we especially need to thank a variety of people for their influence and help in the completion of this book. First, we thank our children—Aubrie, Chase, Tyson, and Kasse for their support, patience, and, most importantly, for being our greatest teachers. In addition, we thank our parents, the late Allan N. and Helen Adams, Dale Huffaker, and Carol Huffaker for teaching us about work and how to impact the world for the better.

In the Maxcomm world, we thank all of out colleagues for their input and suggestions. In particular, our thanks go to Emil Bohn for his constant support and encouragement to keep on working.

We are grateful to the leaders who have embraced out work and allowed us to partner with them in their organizations. We feel blessed and privileged to have had the opportunity to work with some of the finest leaders in the world who consistently achieve results and value the people with whom they are associated. Among those leaders are: Stephen Ewing, Al Pino, Richard Bastian, Allan Nagle, Cliff Dodd, Richard Johnson, Rudy Cifolelli, Scott Slaymaker, Larry Payne, W. A. (Mac) McGriff, Joseph Kanfer, Mark Lerner, Sharon Guten, and Barbara Kuby.

Our thanks to Michael Bowker for providing us with both his writing talent and enthusiasm. He has been a true partner in this project. Most importantly, we are forever grateful to Marjean Daniels, our editor and dear friend. If not for her, this book would not be a reality.

To Executive Excellence Publishing, especially to our editor Ken Shelton, our appreciation for having the patience, belief, and perseverance to see this project through.

Finally, we must thank God, our Creator, for the gift of life itself and without whom, for us, thriving would not be possible. As the author of our faith and the center of our universe, to Him we are thankful for a full and rich life.

—*Bill and Cindy Adams*

Contents

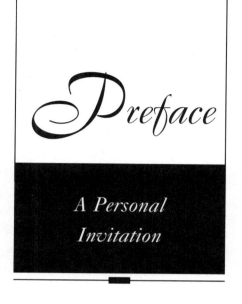

Preface

A Personal Invitation

Please consider this book as our personal invitation to join us on a journey toward a new organization—one where motivated employees drive maximum productivity. Now, more than ever, corporations are under continual pressure to change in ways that better prepare them to compete in the new global economy. In this book, we do more than describe a process for creating an inspiring, motivating corporate culture that works in harmony with evolving business systems and controls. We also present the reasons why we believe the way work is presently viewed and understood must shift completely.

Unlike many change approaches available in the marketplace today, this approach is highly personal in nature. For positive change to be sustained over time, people cannot be viewed as inanimate objects, numbers, or departmental cogs in a wheel. People—the heart, soul, and source of all productivity within organizations—cannot be "engineered." Quantum leaps in productivity do not come from downsizing or acquiring new hardware—hardware which the competition will have in a short time, anyway—but from winning over the hearts, minds, and passionate loyalty of the people who work for the organization.

To fully present this approach to you, we begin by sharing the experiences that ultimately led us to develop what we have termed *The Whole Systems Approach*^{SM}. We chose the name "Whole Systems" carefully because it reflects what will be required of organizations in the future. As we all move from the Information Age into the

Integration Age, business success will depend on how effectively organizations use, leverage, and combine all the resources available to them—particularly the passion, motivation, experience, and wisdom of their greatest asset—people.

Can We Still Change the World?

Much of the ardor we feel about the work of increasing organizational effectiveness is due to the timing of the first line of Baby Boomers lighting 50 candles on their birthday cakes. Some 25 years ago, as a budding generation, we expected to change the world. "Of course we can make a difference!" we thought. "And we will!"

As we entered the workforce and began our families, the reality was that changing the world soon took a back seat to changing jobs and diapers. Many of us spent the next 20 years working to support our families in positions that were not as fulfilling as we had envisioned. Time has eroded the faith, optimism, and ideals we once held.

As we Baby Boomers head into middle age, a new inquiry is beginning to surface within our sizable generation. Having lived in the work environment and practiced the ethics left to us by our parents, we are now, for the first time, considering the legacy of work we will leave for our children.

Can People Thrive at Work?

Imagine how you will feel if one day you go to work and find your entire company has changed. The leadership in the company has moved from being power brokers, concerned mainly with their spans of control, to a higher ground where their primary role is to help employees recognize and express their latent, inherent potential as workers and human beings. You find everyone in the company is excited about their work. Clock watchers are a thing of the past. Employees and management share a mutual respect and value each other's abilities, ideas, and feelings. The prosperity of everyone within the company is a top priority.

To your amazement, you find political posturing and blame labeling—once rampant in the organization—have been replaced by a total commitment to open, truthful communication and finding workable solutions. You are further astonished when you realize people skilled in teamwork, coaching, and communication are the ones being rewarded rather than those adept at office politics. You can scarcely believe that your entire organization has embraced change as a positive partner to creativity and productivity. You actually have to sit down, take a deep breath, and check for a pulse when you observe that every person in your organization has been given accountability and is exercising their voice in making decisions that affect their own work and the future of the organization.

At this point, you feel a little like Alice in Wonderland when she slipped down the rabbit hole. You witness the "cover-your-tail" mentality in your organization has been replaced by a universal and relentless desire to create value for the customer. At the same time, every person within your company now views the fiscal health of the organization as their own personal responsibility. They understand the company as a living thing that must be nurtured in order to grow and thrive.

You begin to realize that what you see is not your company of old, but a community of people with shared goals, working in a cooperative, inspiring, and fulfilling culture. Executives, managers, and employees alike act with immediacy and demonstrate passion for their work, as though they realize they finally have the opportunity to reach their utmost potential!

One thing keeps coming to mind as you try to absorb all these changes—you sense with your head, heart, and soul that your company is about to experience explosive growth and soaring productivity. You recognize you are looking at what seems like a miracle—a world of work where people thrive in an organization that realizes outrageous results.

By now, of course, you may be dismissing this vision as just so much fantasy. You may figure we belong with Alice in that rabbit hole, along with the Cheshire Cat and the Mad Hatter. Or, perhaps you feel this all might be plausible somewhere—on some other planet perhaps—but certainly not where you work!

Why not? What is there to keep this change from happening? If you doubt this change could ever occur, consider this possibility: Does an organization that daily robs its members of their strength, spirit, vision, vitality, sense of community, and passion have a strong future? What about one that creates an environment where people are rewarded for "going outside the box," "owning their results," self-awareness, teamwork, and individual and collective creativity? One where communication is free-flowing, and excitement electrifies the entire corporate environment?

Which of these two organizations is going to thrive? In which would you rather work? The answers seem obvious. Yet, if the choice to work in the second one is so obvious, why is it so hard to conceive of this as the organization of the future? Why is it so difficult to believe we can successfully change corporations in that direction—right now? Why is it so many organizations continue to more closely resemble the first example rather than the second?

Leaving a Legacy

Answering these questions is part of the sense of urgency we feel. The approach we have developed is meant to be a significant positive contribution to a legacy, crystallizing our dreams in today's reality. Beyond just telling you about this approach, we want you to share the same excitement and passion we felt as we journeyed down the path of discovery. The first section of this book chronicles our personal journey and logic for including various aspects of current theories and practices. In the second section, the components of this approach are discussed in a simple, organized framework. The third and final section describes why this approach works, how it can contribute to a new legacy of work, and the keys to manifesting inherent potential.

Our bottom line is about creating and running an outstanding, enduring organization—one that will meet the challenges, seize the opportunities, and ultimately blow the doors off the competition in the new global marketplace. Our top line—highest goal—is to leave a powerful legacy for our children and our children's children. Your participation and engagement could ultimately help lead us toward realizing this magnificent promise we can make to future generations: "Welcome to a world of work where people thrive."

We could not offer this pledge and would not make this vow if we had not realized the possibility ourselves through our experiences in changing and running organizations. Although this book is about business, the process of writing it turned out to be far more personal than we ever could have imagined it would be. Looking back, though, it makes perfect sense. *The Whole Systems Approach* is a direct outgrowth of our personal experiences and beliefs—in other words, who we've become. It is the outcome of our dream to transform the workplace into a stimulating environment where people are valued and can thrive while their companies restore, maintain, and increase their competitive vigor.

This book is about articulating our vision and demonstrating how that vision can be turned into a reality. We are excited to share the process in this book. With the help and commitment of visionary and courageous corporate leaders with whom we've been fortunate to work over the past 15 years, we have proven it is possible to create companies where profitability and fulfillment can peacefully coexist! Hopefully, in the near future, your company will be one of these.

We invite you to pull up the anchor, unfurl the sails, and travel with us as we journey to a new vision of work because that vehicle must be seaworthy enough to carry a vital cargo through some potentially stormy seas. The cargo, of course, is your company. We're slipping into the nautical metaphor here because there's a quote we want to share with you that is a powerful indicator of the human spirit and potential: "A ship is safe in the harbor, but that's not why ships are built." This aphorism captures the attitude we hope you can feel in this book, and in applying *The Whole Systems Approach*. It is an attitude of hope, belief, and tremendous faith in our ability as human beings to create a vision, then sail forth and seek that vision out. It's about the courage to dream and the courage to change. Anchors aweigh!

> —Bill and Cindy Adams
> Salt Lake City, Utah,
> February 1999

Section

I

*The Search
for
What Works*

> "I don't like work—no person does—but I like what is in work—the chance to find yourself."
> —*Joseph Conrad*

Chapter 1

The Grim Reality: Why Work Is a Four-Letter Word

Most businesses today are facing a stiff challenge. Confronted with sharply increasing global competition, customer quality demands, and an overabundance of available data, these businesses must adapt quickly or be left behind. Yet, too many companies are either resisting change or going about it in a way that cannot achieve the desired results. Senior leaders are frustrated and overwhelmed with the enormity of the issues their organizations face without a clear path to resolution. Many managers often dig in their heels like mules at the word "change" because of what "change" represents and how it has affected them over the last decade. Or, they decide to play the game and go so far as to hire consultants to give the impression they are promoting change, but this is little more than lip service. For many, charade or real, meaningful change has become a joke, and the best that can be said is, "Well, that change experiment is over. Now we can go back to business as usual."

During our early years as consultants, we conducted ongoing research into every change approach being employed in organizations around the world. It became evident that as we were committing to creating a world of work where individuals and organizations could thrive—a Camelot at Work—many people were becoming highly cynical about the workplace. "What!" they practically shouted at us:

"Personal fulfillment at work? Excitement and passion, too? A sense of community among my fellow workers? Realizing my inherent potential at work? Who are you kidding? Not in this lifetime!"

We found too many employees and managers were resigned to being unfulfilled in their jobs. They did not believe personal satisfaction would ever be possible at their workplace. Even worse, many felt that was the way work was supposed to feel—it was supposed to be full of drudgery and pain. We also discovered an equally discouraging fact regarding management attitudes. It became clear that most senior leaders did not appreciate the fact that motivated employees will, by far, out-produce those who are not motivated. It seems like common sense—if people are excited about their work, they are naturally going to work smarter, and more creatively and efficiently, than those who cannot wait to escape work at any opportunity.

To achieve a state of maximum productivity, people must be motivated, inspired, and personally connected to the work they do. This productive state can be realized, in part, by giving employees a voice in how they do their work. Equally important is the establishment of innovative business systems that support each individual while allowing the company to maximize its investment potential and bottom-line performance.

Unfortunately, for many employees, *work* is a four-letter word. More people know *TGIF* better than *e pluribus unum*. A large majority of workers neither like their jobs nor feel connected to their work products or services. Given this reality, the question quickly becomes, "Are we realizing maximum productivity from people who feel this way?" The answer is a resounding "No!"

Nearly everyone agrees change is needed; however, relatively few meaningful efforts to change the status quo have been carried out. On the surface, leaders often appear to act in a cavalier manner; however, deep down, they too are grappling like the rest of us to find something that will make a difference. To understand this powerful reluctance to change, we must first explore the history of how and when *work* became a four-letter word.

Once a Nation of Home-Based Businesses

Most of our great-grandparents grew up working in or owning small businesses, many in the form of farms and ranches. Although sharecropping was an exception, most farmers owned the land they worked. At one time, we were, in effect, a nation of self-employed people. There was no hierarchy at work because farmers, ranchers, and those skilled in a trade answered only to themselves and, of course, to the weather. No one told them when to be at work or what their job descriptions were. The need for staff memos, "mandatory"meetings, annual reviews, probationary periods, or requests for raises did not exist. Our great-grandparents did not work solely for a paycheck; in fact, it was just the reverse. The fruits of their labor literally sustained them. They were directly linked to the product of their work and, by extension, to their community.

Industrialization changed this model. With the proliferation of factories and retail outlets, young people were soon lured away to work for someone else. Almost overnight, we ceased to be a nation of home-based businesses. The majority of workers left their homes every morning to labor for others. They were no longer in charge of their own time. As a result, a whole new work structure and attitude evolved. Rather than producing something that sustained them, people were working for a means to that end. For the first time, people were separated from the actual product of their work.

As the manufacturing and industrial companies grew larger, the hierarchical concept emerged. Power and decision-making were concentrated in the hands of a few at the top, even though most "hands-on" work was done by the many at the bottom. Disassociated from the product of their work and with no say in decisions about how they did the work, the "employee" mind-set took shape. People started to consider work as a way of trading their time for a paycheck in an arena where they had little or no control.

This top-down hierarchy model viewed organizations as machines and the people who worked in those organizations as cogs in those machines. This organization-as-machine concept was refined by Frederick Winslow Taylor, Henry Ford's organizational consultant. For its time, this concept provided a practical "break-through" solution to a difficult problem—a largely unskilled work-force, many of whom spoke little or no English.

In the hierarchical structure Taylor constructed, each worker was trained to perform one simple task, over and over again. This allowed the organization to circumvent communication problems, as the necessity for workers to talk with each other or to their super-visors was virtually non-existent. The marketplace was not very complex, and the company faced relatively little competition. Therefore, there was no need for the company to be adaptive, flex-ible, or creative. Taylor's system, in fact, discouraged creativity. Any deviation by the workers from their tightly defined assignments threatened the entire vertical structure.

At the top of the hierarchy was the boss, who oversaw the oper-ation from a position literally above the workers who were located on the ground floor and were neither required nor encouraged to understand the "big picture." As long as each worker mastered a single task, the production scheme worked, and automobiles rolled off the assembly line.

Taylor's mechanistic paradigm proved so successful that it was copied and emulated by organizations worldwide. Unfortunately, the top-down hierarchy eventually evolved into business concepts that are now outdated, such as:

- Organizations perceived as emotionless machines made of detachable parts
- Workers given only narrowly defined roles and tasks
- Employee motivation generated by external forces
- All decisions made by the "boss"
- Fear used as a management tool
- Information shared among management only
- Change as an anathema to be avoided

As an evolutionary outgrowth of the Ford-Taylor model, employ-ees were deterred from taking the initiative to solve any problems on their own. Companies avoided risks at all cost and, as a result, grew inflexible and unable to adapt quickly. This super-conservative structure, based on unquestioned obedience to a hierarchical chain of authority, was, for many of our parents, the legacy left to them. The paradigm has pervaded our view of the world around us. In its time, it was a powerful concept that produced hundreds of thousands of automobiles, all the same color and style. But like the Model Ts that rolled down the old assembly lines, this organization-as-machine approach is an anachronism that is clearly out of place in today's world.

I'm Okay! You're Okay! (But I'm still the boss!)

After World War II, experts in the United States and England began studying work dynamics within organizations. Consultants at the Tavistock Institute in London encouraged business leaders to give workers more responsibility. Similarly, experts at Boston's Massachusetts Institute of Technology developed a new theory based on sensitivity training called the T-group. This new focus on the personal growth of the worker developed slowly during the 1950s and '60s. The human potential movement, as it came to be known, was based on enhancing the quality of life for workers and concerned itself only incidentally with the quality of the product.

The political and social turbulence of the late 1960s and early '70s helped shift the human potential movement into high gear. Long-established ideas of how organizations had been run in the past were questioned. The country began looking inward in an effort to heal the psychic wounds left by the Vietnam War while books like *I'm Okay! You're Okay!* rose to the top of the bestseller list. Personal growth advocates gained credibility by capturing huge consulting contracts from major companies. For the first time, leaders were encouraged to listen instead of just command. Communication with employees was recommended, and conflict resolution became a primary leadership responsibility. By the early 1970s, management training had become big business.

Although the aim of the human potential movement was altruistic, it was a setup and doomed to failure from the get-go. The movement stressed the values of participation and personal growth but did nothing to change the top-down hierarchy in organizations.

All meaningful decisions within companies were still made solely by leaders and managers. Employees were told to think for themselves and act independently; yet, they were stifled by the same paralyzing layers of bureaucracy that created a need for the human potential movement in the first place. Full employee participation remained a myth, and, in many cases, the hypocrisy cost management much of its credibility.

The Quality Revolution

The human potential movement did accomplish one important goal—it helped nurture the Baby Boomer generation's belief that personal fulfillment is a birthright. It raised expectations that the workplace could be a creative, fulfilling arena. The concept remained alive into the 1980s, even as the marketplace itself was undergoing dynamic, rapid shifts.

As Japan and other countries began to muscle in on the world marketplace, which had been dominated by the U.S. since World War II, American companies found themselves in the fight of their lives. When Japanese manufacturers swept past their American counterparts in the sale of electronics, automobiles, and other products, American companies began to challenge the slow-moving, hierarchical structures of their own organizations.

Around the same time, American consumers were demanding higher quality products. In 1978, only 30 percent of the respondents in a U.S. consumer poll indicated they considered quality more important than price when purchasing a product or service. A similar poll taken in 1990 showed a dramatic shift in attitudes among American consumers. More than 70 percent now said that quality was more important than price. All at once, organizations were not only faced with greater competition, but with meeting a higher product and service standard as well.

Parallel to the quality movement was a new generation of thinking that went beyond the human potential movement. In their book *In Search of Excellence*, Tom Peters and Robert Waterman vigorously attacked traditional corporate attitudes toward employees.

"American corporations treat employees like children," Peters thundered. "Why, we even have to ask permission to go to the bathroom! Is this any way to run a business?"

Ken Blanchard expanded on Peter's broad concept in his book *The One-Minute Manager.* In this short but compelling book, Blanchard suggested a heretofore unique way to manage people. Investing quality time with people, establishing high expectations and goals, and building trust and teamwork through reinforcement rather than punishment were all powerful new ideas for the times. Blanchard helped validate the concept that management needed to nurture employees to ensure their organization's survival.

These books and others, like Sisyphus's stone rolling down the hill, began to build momentum and provide a serious alternative to the traditional company-as-machine mentality. *The Fifth Discipline* by Peter Senge, *Productive Workplaces* by Marvin Weisbord, and *Leadership Is an Art* by Max DePree all added fuel to the fire. In *The 7 Habits of Highly Effective People*, Stephen R. Covey succeeded in legitimizing the whole person and championed spirit and spirituality in the workplace.

Even with these revolutionary ideas and publication of these groundbreaking books, many workers still viewed *work* as a four-letter word—something they did to earn a living rather than as an expression of their life's purpose. Clearly, earning a living is a necessity; however, our inquiry became, "If you could have both, why wouldn't you take both?"

We began our pursuit for improving organizational effectiveness as enthusiastic, but inexperienced, college graduates moving into the corporate world. We expected to find internal cultures that were mature, wise, confident, nourishing, and structured around what was in the best interest of both people and profitability. Instead, we discovered corporate power structures that often fostered the opposite environments—ones that were de-motivating, fear-laden, and stifling; whose employees felt disenfranchised to the point of being openly hostile toward their employers; and where productivity was nowhere near what it could or should be.

Chapter

2

A Voyage of Discovery

The Face of Failure

Like most of our classmates, we left graduate school with the common perception that Corporate America knew how to motivate people to do their best work to secure the organization's future. It did not take long before our hopeful idealism came crashing down around us. Even though we lost our naiveté along the way, we still believed it was possible to create a world of work where both people and companies could thrive. We were neither ready nor willing to relinquish our dreams so easily, no matter how many examples we encountered to the contrary. Even an intangible concept can become a powerful vision if the belief is strong enough.

BILL: One of my first jobs was working for a large insurance company as an internal consultant. Management was trying to implement some significant changes. The management team had announced a new plan that included well-designed training and compensation programs, an outstanding performance appraisal system, and excellent hiring practices. Management also promised a team-building process in which the front-line people would participate to become an integral part of the decision-making process.

Six months into the effort, it was clear something was wrong. We were failing. We were experiencing a high turnover rate, particularly with our newest employees. The dilemma kept me awake nights. Then, in a casual meeting, I connected with a real person who was a victim of the company's supposedly wonderful new ideals. It was then I first began to understand the concept of the organization as a living system. Seven of us were in a meeting—three managers, three front-line employees, and me. One of the front-line employees, Tom, was a bright young man with a promising future at the company. However, he was also very frustrated. Six weeks earlier, Tom's team had made specific recommendations on some changes the team felt should be made within the company. None of the changes had been implemented, nor had he or the team received any word regarding these recommendations from management.

Toward the end of the meeting, Tom inquired as to the fate of his team's recommendations. The senior manager stood and smiled. "As you know, Tom, we appreciate and encourage all input from employees," he said. "Unfortunately, this suggestion did not fit with what we have in mind. But, please, anything else you might think of in the future, let us know." Seated across from Tom, I watched him as his face registered disbelief, then disappointment, and finally contempt. For a company trying to win the hearts and minds of its employees, it was the face of failure!

Less than a month later, Tom left the company, taking his training and considerable skills and talent with him. Before he left, I had an opportunity to speak with him. "The problem is management still sees employees as part of the machinery to be maneuvered however it deems necessary," Tom told me. "There has been a lot of rhetoric from senior leadership about how we're all going to be involved, but the fact is, we employees have been shut out of the loop."

It was clear why the organization was not doing as well as it could have. The company had worked hard at each individual component, such as training, compensation, appraisal systems, hiring practices, and the like, but the components never completely came together. Each was considered separately and not fully integrated into an organic whole.

The "Big Lie"

Tom's situation is not an isolated incident. In company after company, leadership's rhetoric does not match the reality of the employees' day-to-day experiences. Organizations constantly espouse one set of values while living another. The rhetoric of full participation, however, continues to appear in annual reports, internal communications, vision and value statements, and the speeches given by senior leaders—as if full participation were the reality.

The hypocrisy has created an open wound with the employees. Leadership says, "People are our most valued asset." Yet, every employee knows they are vulnerable to downsizing and layoffs if "the numbers aren't right." Leadership talks about "teamwork," while each individual must fight to protect himself or herself while clinging to the corporate ladder. Leadership talks about pushing decision-making to the "lowest possible level" (just listen to the bias in that language of the "lowest possible level"), while everybody knows the important decisions always come from the top.

The fact is, management would be better served by telling the truth: "The *boss* makes *all* the decisions; you employees are *not* our most valued assets; we will *fire you* if the numbers aren't right; teamwork is a *myth*; and everything—including quality—can and will be *sacrificed* for *short-term profit!*"

As painful as it would be, employees could live with that kind of honesty more easily than they can swallow the insidious lies they are being told over and over. A whole contingent of skeptics and cynics are resident inside our corporations. Any meaningful change can only be driven by the truth. The rhetoric has to equal the reality. No one will accept a change driven only from the top. Real change, honest change—change that employees believe, support, and buy into—has to fully involve them and the "whole system," including stakeholders, vendors, and customers.

Disillusioned and Disappointed

CINDY: My goal, when I started college, was to be a dancer, marry, and have children. I had watched my father grow to hate his job as a lawyer and wasn't sure the corporate world was for me. My father was an idealist in the high-pressure, contentious, and often bitter world of family law. He worked everyday in a hostile environment that would have even robbed idealism from Gandhi. Dad was frequently miserable and depressed by the time he finally came home from work, which was often late in the evening. I remember tiptoeing past his den late at night and seeing him leaning back in his chair, staring at the wall, his fingers rubbing his temples. Even at a young age, I knew there was something wrong with that image. I grew up feeling uneasy about the world of work.

Still, I took on several full- and part-time jobs to save money for college and, eventually, worked my way through graduate school. One such organization where I worked was a local bank. To my surprise, I found I enjoyed the financial business world. I was soon promoted, and, at 20 years of age, I realized there was a certain measure of satisfaction one could find in work. I gained confidence and began, for the first time, to dream of a career as a professional.

One such career move was an opportunity to help direct a federal program in Salt Lake City called Projects with Industry. A very amenable person named Van Potter hired me away from the bank and served as my mentor for several years. He treated me as a partner from the moment I was hired and showed me it was possible to be inspired, motivated, and passionate about work. He gave me free rein to build the business and encouraged me to the point where I began to believe strongly in my own abilities and in my own right to be fulfilled by my work.

Our mission at Projects with Industry was to prepare physically challenged workers for employment and to train corporate leaders in how to treat and gain the maximum effort from these workers. As Van's own son had cerebral palsy, he was extremely passionate about our work. I shared his passion. As I worked with corporate leaders, I believed they knew what they were doing and understood the people who worked for them. I found the opposite was the case. I was amazed to learn that most companies are filled with barriers that actually keep employees from reaching their full potential. As a result, many people in those companies become resigned and effectively quit. The workers we talked with as we were assisting teams in accepting and working with the disabled often discussed openly their strategies for expending only the minimum energy necessary to do the work and still keep their jobs.

What I observed was that not only did the employees and managers suffer from varying degrees of low morale and a perpetual lack of self-esteem, but many corporations and their leaders also suffered from low levels of self-esteem. By "low self-esteem," I mean they did not believe they deserved "work happiness," nor did they feel confident their contribution was truly valuable and valued. Many companies, as a whole, were, in fact, depressed and didn't inspire much hope for a bright, doable future.

This experience lit the "fire in my belly" to help make a difference because I realized the corporate world knew very little about what it was doing with regard to its people. As I searched for a sense of community and "spirit" within these organizations, I discovered little of either. Most corporate leaders just shrugged when I brought up the subject. Many simply ignored me, labeling community and spirit as irrelevant "female" concerns. Yet, a feeling of community—the sense that the people around you care about you—hardly qualifies as a gender issue; it goes to the heart of open communication, cooperation, motivation, fulfillment, confidence, and a dozen other factors that affect a person's work and influence an organization's overall effectiveness and productivity.

As I was becoming disillusioned by corporate attitudes, I was also experiencing positive growth in my own position. We effectively formed a sanctuary within the governmental organization to which we were accountable. Van was one of those visionary leaders who protected his employees while giving them responsibility and a say over their own work. As a result, we thrived as a unit. Surrounded by hopeless tangles of bureaucracy, our unit nevertheless performed at a threateningly high level. We were total renegades within this creaking, suffocating system, which was why our results were consistently the highest among other government agencies engaged in the same work.

I grew increasingly disheartened with the world of work I encountered outside of our little unit. Whenever I entered a new company, I would conduct an informal poll among the employees. My first question was: "What percentage of your waking hours do you spend at work?" Most people said they spent more than half their waking hours on the job. I then inquired if they were happy at work. Fewer than 20 percent of the employees I talked with indicated they felt fulfilled or inspired by their work!

The implications of these responses stunned me. Most of these employees—I polled thousands of them over the years—spent the majority of their lives in an environment where they felt unfulfilled and less than happy. What a waste! One frustrated executive described his situation this way: "The time I'm putting into this organization is literally my life's blood. The hours I spend here in my office are deducted from my life. How can I possibly justify spending it here if I'm not doing something meaningful?"

I find many people are making that trade, but not willingly with a full heart or all their energy. The situation is not only unhealthy for the individuals, but for their organizations as well. Although organizations may survive in a diseased state, they cannot thrive. Most leaders of these organizations wanted to inspire their employees, but the truth was, many were failures at it. I couldn't accept this reality. I, along with many others, knew there had to be a better way and began my own search for what could and would work.

Work as Fulfillment

BILL: My understanding of work sprang from growing up on a cattle ranch on the Utah/Wyoming border. My father loved being a rancher; his work was his passion. His father, my grandfather, operated a large bank and wanted his sons to follow him into the business world. My father tried the banking business for a while, but his heart was not in that work. He loved being outdoors and wanted to be in the ranching business.

At age 25, with his father's reluctant blessing, my father left the bank and went to work with my great-grandfather. Eventually, he ended up owning his own ranch. As almost any rancher can tell you, raising cattle is an up-and-down business. Times weren't always smooth for us. Whenever things got rough and problems closed in on my father, he would always go outside and find some work to do—putting up fences, moving cattle, or tending to the horses. His actions taught me a valuable lesson. Rather than seeking escape from his work when he felt pressured, my father sought out work because it was his comfort—his solace. Work was not what he did to live; it was what he lived to do. He taught me that there was no separation between work and life. We didn't go home after work; our work was our home.

I grew up with a profound love and respect for work. I believed work nourished me and made me stronger and better. When I was young, I assumed everybody shared the same perception. Later, I discovered those who do are the exception, rather than the rule. It appeared to me then—as it still does—that something was out of whack. For example, after graduate school, I went to work at a company in the South. One of the jobs I had was to teach and coach a group of hipods—young recruits who had earned the nickname because management considered these individuals to be "high potential" leadership candidates.

I was so energized that I could barely contain my enthusiasm. My first job had presented me with the opportunity of a lifetime. Management articulated that total participation, involvement, and a full exchange of information within the company were not only expected, but demanded of the employees. I was assured every employee had a voice over his or her own work processes. It all sounded wonderful to me. However, a short time after joining the company, I realized the promises were a desire not yet realized. Much of the top management talked a good game but did not encourage participation, involvement, or communication. The CEO set the opposite example by cloaking himself within a small group of people, who were themselves constantly out of his favor. He was demanding in a way that prevented people working near him from finding satisfaction in their own work. He ran his company like a kingdom, and he was the king.

After a few months inside the organization, during which much of my innocence about corporations fell by the wayside, I began to notice something peculiar. As an internal consultant, I virtually had the run of the entire company. I began to watch as many people continually sought transfers to small pockets within the company. My curiosity was piqued; I began to check out what was going on. In every instance, I found these small units were headed up by progressive leaders who resolutely protected their employees from top managers.

I learned these small pockets of "safe areas" were known around the company as "refugee camps." In these "camps," people could escape the negative culture that prevailed in the rest of the organization. The progressive leaders who supervised these "camps" were invariably the ones who actually acted out the rhetoric espoused by top management. They truly did foster trust, participation, mutual respect, a free flow of information, and a fear-free environment where innovation and risk-taking were encouraged and rewarded. The most important aspect of these refugee camps was that they were always the most productive units within the company. That fact underscored my growing awareness that people cannot be separated from their work without greatly reducing their overall effectiveness and productivity.

After several years, I went to work for a multinational, privately-held company with 35,000 employees. The company was a holding company for 33 subsidiary corporations. I felt it was a perfect environment for me because there were so many opportunities to observe and work with different corporate cultures. Still in my 20s, I was placed in charge of organizational development for the entire organization. Specifically, I headed up training and organizational development—another one of my dream jobs.

The dream, though, soon turned into a nightmare. I had learned from my prior job that it is possible to do your best work and reach your maximum productivity only when your personal values are aligned with those of the company. When these values coincide, a synergy occurs that adds motivation, inspiration, and even joy to the work. But if those values do not align, passion is stilled, and vast amounts of energy are either lost or consumed in the struggle to justify the discrepancy. I quickly learned my own values were completely out of alignment with those of the company.

First, most of the employees were minimum wage earners who were not valued as individuals by top management. As a result, few employees were high producers. They felt little enthusiasm for or loyalty to the company. Most felt the company was trying to "rip them off" and many carried a chip on their shoulders. The turnover rate was high, and it was frustrating to deal with the low employee morale. The real problem, though, was management's attitude. They hated unions and spent a great deal of time and effort either avoiding unionization or trying to bust the existing unions. It was constant warfare—exactly the reverse of the environment I felt should be fostered by management.

During this experience, it became crystal clear that leaders are completely in charge of their companies. Whatever the owners and CEOs want, they get. I found that when my own values came in direct conflict with the way the company was run, I wasn't able to do my best work. I constantly found myself at odds with what I felt was a vicious way to run a company. Besides running against my ethical and moral beliefs, I didn't believe, in the long run, such a soulless, uninspiring work culture could allow the company to reach its full financial potential.

Early on, I also had developed a bias that people wanted to involve themselves in their work by having a say in how the work was done. While I was working on the ranch with my father, he often not only told me what to do, but how to do it, even though I had been the one doing that specific task for many years. It frustrated me because I had fine-tuned my efforts to do the job in the fastest and most effective way possible. However, Dad was very strong-willed and insisted I do it "his way." I would be putting up hay in a certain way with great results when my dad would walk in and tell me to fork the hay up in another way I already knew was less effective. I lost ownership of my own efforts; it made me hopping mad. Dad and I would subsequently fight like cats and dogs. I would then waste the rest of the day being mad at Dad and not being as effective as I could be.

What drove me in those days was my experience as a corporate manager. I learned that truthfulness is not necessarily valued within companies. People want to hear what is safe. As a result, too many people inside organizations never tell the truth. Yet, for whatever reason, top management will often accept the truth from an outside source. I saw that external consultants had a tremendous advantage in working directly with senior leaders and the CEO to get things done. As a consultant, I had the keys to the playground and could have a more significant impact than I was able to have from inside the corporation.

My desire to have an impact led me to a crossroads. I had been working for many years inside corporations and had learned a great deal. I started my work believing management's rhetoric and left realizing that serious change was necessary before "the talk" matched the reality within most corporations. At the same time, I also began to realize that corporations would need outside help if they were to change on the inside. This formidable challenge had to come from the inside with help from the outside, and the outside was where I needed to be.

During this time, I had several long conversations with Emil Bohn, who had been my professor and mentor when I was doing undergraduate work. I greatly respected Emil as an educator. Over the years, we had kept in touch and occasionally talked about starting a business together. It seemed to be the perfect opportunity to open the business about which we had talked. In October 1984, Emil and I founded Maxcomm. We were busy from the start. We quickly landed contracts with federal and local governments as well as with my old company, which hired us to make the changes I had tried to make from the inside.

Over the next decade, Maxcomm flourished as we worked with clients all over the world covering all industries. Much of what Emil and I did in those earlier days is still meeting the test of time. One single concept remained clear and led us like a lighthouse beacon. That concept was: *People will support what they help to create.*

Although this is not a complex idea, it is quite profound. When people take ownership for a change, that change usually works. If they don't, it can take years to convince them to accept it; of course, some never will. We felt then, as we do now, that the involvement of all people within the organization is the key to positive and enduring change.

Over time, we tinkered with, modified, and developed strategies based on our successes while incorporating what we learned from the failures. This was a new field, a new art form, and everybody was experimenting with new ideas.

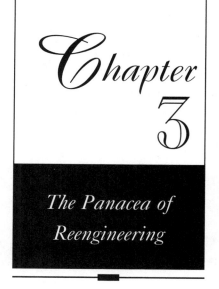

Chapter 3

The Panacea of Reengineering

In 1991, we were in the midst of two major change efforts that had been ongoing for several years. Both efforts were successful based on client results and customer feedback. Our models had been repeatedly field tested and refined. However, given the speed of technological advancement, we felt we were missing something big that could create a significant shift in our approach and greatly reduce our cycle time while preserving our belief in the value of the individual.

We were encouraged when thinkers and leaders such as Tom Peters, Peter Drucker, Rosabeth Moss Kanter, and others began to encourage corporations to focus on their customers and employees. These pathfinders made our jobs as practitioners in the daunting field of organizational change much easier. Some went a step further and urged corporate leaders to surrender new powers and decision-making responsibilities to front-line employees and their work teams. Arguments arose over which should come first—the focus on customers or the realignment of decision-making power.

The Promise of Reengineering

A far more significant dispute surfaced over how to change the organization. Michael Hammer, James Champy, and others convinced most of the corporate world that reengineering was "the" answer. The concept of reengineering appealed to traditionalists, who champion management-dictated changes in operations and whose primary focus has always been, and continues to be, on bottom-line numbers. The prime objective of the traditionalists is the absolute control of these numbers. The strategies of reengineering fit perfectly into a mind-set that views organizations as mechanical operations that can be reengineered or fixed by simply replacing any or all of the parts, including employees.

A critical element of the reengineering approach is the need for swift action. However it is to be accomplished, the demolition of the old has to be planned and executed by the top ranks of leadership with breakneck speed. The result is far from bloodless—the horrors of downsizing sprang from what companies executed as a "meat cleaver" approach. Yet, reengineering promised a quick and simple solution, kept top management in control of the ship and, most importantly, pleased Wall Street. For these reasons, reengineering captured the interest of most of the corporate world and became the change approach of choice. As Peter Drucker observed, "Reengineering is new, and it has to be done."

We found our own beliefs were in alignment with much of what Hammer and Champy were proposing. In fact, we had been practicing their primary theme—that companies must organize work around process—for several years. Hammer and Champy accurately noted that a major problem within modern corporations was that there was no one in charge of the processes necessary to produce goods or services. "In fact," they wrote, "hardly anyone is even aware of them." We felt this was a powerful and urgent message to send to organizations. We applauded when Hammer and Champy noted that "the industrial model rests on the basic premise that workers have few skills and little time or capacity for training. The premise inevitably requires that the jobs and tasks assigned to these workers be very simple. . . . In reengineering, we stand (that) industrial model on its head."

Even though many of the reengineering philosophies seemed to support our major tenet that people—employees—were a great untapped resource within most corporations, we had long witnessed management's perception of workers as having few skills, little imagination, no problem-solving abilities, and even less passion about their work as a self-fulfilling prophecy. Few employees will flourish in a culture that does not support them. We hoped reengineering would help raise the awareness of leaders to that fact.

We were further encouraged when Hammer and Champy described the new roles and opportunities for workers—especially when they called for employees to have a greater decision-making voice. "Employee empowerment" was the buzzword, and we, of course, supported it. They wrote convincingly of installing processes and systems that promoted employee recognition and involvement. All these things—a focus on process, employee involvement, and supporting management systems—were consistent with the principles upon which we had based Maxcomm nearly a decade before.

We found Hammer and Champy's philosophy of starting over with a "clean slate" and the possibility for "radical" change to be sound; however, we disagreed with certain aspects of their approach. Unfortunately, in the end, reengineering contained one fatal flaw that surfaced when the authors addressed *who* would reengineer? At that point, the entire process fell apart. Hammer and Champy recommended the reengineering itself be done by a small team of elite managers and outside consultants. This crack team was to make the sweeping changes necessary to turn the company into a process-oriented organization. The authors went so far as to endorse the appointment of a "reengineering czar," or "leg breaker," who would run the entire process. They also supported a senior manager who said: "We concluded early in the game that this was a top-down process, not something that was likely to reach critical mass on its own or something that would bubble up." With those words, we knew the majority of reengineering efforts would fail!

Reengineering Abused

Implementation of reengineering became a problem as scores of leaders and big name consultants began attempting, in one form or another, to reengineer organizations. Most of them took a potentially good tool—reorganizing around processes—and badly abused it. The majority of change efforts focused solely on the labor-saving potential of the new process and technology. The emphasis was almost entirely on how to cut employee numbers through changing processes and adding automation. It was a move initially applauded by Wall Street; companies began to see their stock value soar in direct relationship to the number of employees they could eliminate. The human elements of the reengineering concept were ignored, and organizations were seen as mechanisms to be "fixed," much like an automobile or appliance in need of repair. It was the total corruption of what reengineering was supposed to embrace.

Clearly, organizations characterized by a rigid adherence to top-down authority, limited job roles and responsibilities, ubiquitous boundaries, and a soulless, lifeless core that makes total control from the top seem possible have dismal futures. With no flexibility, speed, or ability to adapt, they cannot possibly keep pace with the realities of today's accelerating, competitive global marketplace. Reengineering did not work most of the time because of the way it was implemented. Top-down control and a total lack of awareness of the need for employee participation were missing components— and the reason these organizations were falling behind the competition in the first place.

Obliterated Loyalty

The results were predictable. All over the world, bottom-line profits of corporations improved over the short-term. Stockholders and investors were momentarily happy. But, an alarming number of employees were dumped unceremoniously into the streets as downsizing, "rightsizing" (now that's an ironic term), and reductions-in-force (RIFs) became the common, albeit fear-inducing, phrases. Social contracts within organizations were obliterated, and the world of work, as we had experienced it growing up, ceased to exist.

Only now are we seeing the beginnings of the long-term fallout from reengineering. Loyalty to an employer, once widespread in this country, has been replaced by cynicism and disloyalty. This was shell-shock for the survivors and the disenfranchised. Corporate trust is almost an oxymoron. "Winning one for the team" is now a statement likely to produce derisive laughter as we've moved

toward the bunker mentality of "every person for him- or herself."
It is a big price to pay. And, for what? In the long run, more than 80
percent of all change efforts are not successful.

A Defensive Posture

Our own experience shows that in company after company, substantial change that is designed and driven entirely from the top-
down rarely succeeds. Everything, from our life and work
experiences to our knowledge of people and just plain common
sense, underscores the reason why. Today, we conduct a simple
exercise to illustrate the basis of our skepticism. We ask for a vol-
unteer or two to join us in front of an audience of participants.
Smiling with anticipation, our unsuspecting volunteers stand facing
us. We leave our volunteers alone for a moment while we address
the audience. We talk about change, organizational health, leadership, and potential, while intentionally ignoring our volunteers.

Our volunteers soon begin to transfer their weight from one foot
to the other, becoming very self-conscious. They're anxious to get
on with their part of the program—whatever that might be. Finally,
it's their turn. We walk across the room, stopping directly in front of
them, and quietly ask their permission to give them a little shove,
just hard enough to make them take a step backward. As we shove
our volunteers, they grin self-consciously as the audience reacts
with laughter and surprise. We push our volunteers a second time.
We repeat the process until our volunteers have marched across the
room backwards, one step at a time.

Before long their smiles fade, and the audience begins to stir
uncomfortably. Finally, our volunteers begin to resist. They dig in
their heels, hold their ground, push back, or move out of the way.
At that point, we end the activity and discuss the point of this exercise. The lesson that once seemed so obvious to us as children is
often forgotten as organizations try to change corporate structure
and culture. The fact is, few of us like to be pushed around. People
instinctively resist change when it's forced upon them!

Without the full cooperation of the people whose lives and jobs you are changing, the chance of "selling" that change to them is greatly diminished. The idea that employees can be "empowered" by assigning senior management to redesign not only their jobs but their values would be laughable if the costs of such a mistaken notion weren't so high. The price not only includes time and money but lost management credibility and personal anguish at all levels.

We are often called in by corporate leaders after a reengineering change effort has failed. They inevitably express great frustration and confusion about why their change efforts are not working. They believe they took all the correct steps. They consulted with experts, personally supervised the change effort, and carefully shared their vision with a select team that drew up a fabulous restructuring plan in record time. Then, with bells, whistles, and hats thrown into the air, the great change was announced to the employees of the company. Meanwhile, within the ranks, the rumor mills worked overtime as these same employees, kept in the dark for months, wondered whether they would have jobs after "the great change" was over. After months of fear and uncertainty, the employees were subjected to management's revelation (as if from *on High*), the *tablets* containing the plan. Like children, the employees—who had no say in any of this—were told how their jobs would change and what their new set of cultural values would be.

It does not take a genius to figure out how employees are going to react. Yet, in most cases, management expressed genuine amazement when the employees responded with something less than excitement, enthusiasm, and total trust in the plan. One CEO, who expressed the sentiments of many others, told us: "It took less than six months for our small senior management team to create the most beautiful change plan you've ever seen. We were all in love with it. Then we spent the next three years trying to sell it to the employees, and I don't think we ever will succeed."

For all their positive contributions, Hammer and Champy ignored one vital principle: *No meaningful change effort will succeed without the full involvement of the people whose lives and jobs you are trying to change.* This is described in science as Ohm's law—with every action, there is an *equal* and *opposite* reaction. If employees are not part of the "action," be prepared!

To his credit, in 1995 Champy came to recognize that reengineering was causing a serious backlash. In his book, *Reengineering Management*, he wrote: "Reengineering is in trouble. It's not easy for me to make this admission. I was one of the two people who introduced the concept. . . . The trouble is, popular concepts sometimes look like magic, and the more popular they become, the more powerful the magic seems."

The problems that the misuse of reengineering has caused are going to be with us for years to come. Between the downsizing and imposed change methods utilized, these efforts have created a huge reservoir of cynicism and anger among hundreds of thousands, if not millions, of employees.

Some even deem these leaders and organizations who have tried reengineering as "bad." Of course, they are not. They were searching for answers to the tremendous problems faced by their organizations; however, many missed a fundamental concept of our time—substantial, permanent leaps in productivity do not come from expensive new hardware, which the competition will have in a few weeks anyway, but from winning over the hearts and minds of the people in the organization!

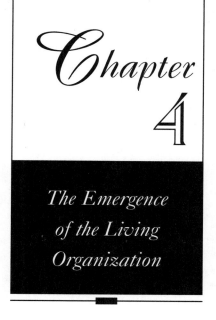

Chapter 4

The Emergence of the Living Organization

As we were studying and testing most of the new organizational change theories and tinkering with our own, we were also under the gun to produce for our clients who were in need of immediate, dramatic, and tangible results. We deliberately sought out all of the "seminal works" published in our fields, explored and scrutinized every resource available, held numerous private and public discussions on the subject of corporate change, participated in scores of seminars, collaborated with many of the leading experts (Hammer, Wheatley, Rummler, Pasmore), and examined the works of Emery, Trist, Senge, and Weisbord, among others.

The speed of change was a driving concern. What emerged for us was more questions: How can we make changes faster, simpler, and more self-sustaining so organizations emerge healthier than they were before? How can we best involve employees in the process so they take ownership for the welfare of the company? How can organizations be consistent, bottom-line performers and still be integrated, process-oriented wholes, rather than fragmented, non-communicating parts? What organizational approach will truly create a competitive advantage?

In 1992, Margaret J. Wheatley's book, *Leadership and the New Science*, rose in prominence alongside Hammer and Champy's *Reengineering the Corporation*. These two books dug battlements at the opposite ends of the corporate change continuum. As businesses were embracing reengineering, thinkers and experimenters like Wheatley emerged with a concept that was diametrically opposed to reengineering. They contended that corporations weren't machines at all, but living organisms, and these living organisms must be allowed to self-organize and adapt, much like a living entity self-organizes and adapts to its environment.

Exploring Self-Organizing Systems

The year before Margaret Wheatley's book was published, we had the good fortune of working closely with her and joint-venturing the first Self-Organizing Systems conferences. During our work with Meg, we learned that organizations must be viewed from a much different perspective than we had viewed them in the past because they were not mechanical, Newtonian things at all.

Even though we had always been on the "people side" of the ledger when it came to understanding organizations, this was a tremendously powerful paradigm shift for us. Wheatley based her approach on the principles found in complexity theory, which assumes that complex, adaptive systems "run" themselves and thus are "self-organizing." According to Wheatley, it is Nature, or more precisely Natural Law, that ultimately provides the hope, vision, and premise that perfection, in terms of full growth attainment, is possible. The self-organizing system proponents favored principles such as living at the "edge of chaos," focusing on the customer, a paramount concern for vision and values, and total elimination of control.

An immense gulf developed between the mechanical and the living organization approaches. On one side was the common management view with a direct lineage back to Sir Isaac Newton, who believed the universe "ran like a clock." If you understood each part, according to Newton, each part, in fact—and therefore the whole—would be predictable, and thus controllable. The result of this view, as applied to our organizations, is an almost military type command-and-control hierarchy. In this top-down view, the people within the organization are seen as depreciating assets—cogs in the wheel that can be changed or eliminated as necessary to make the machine run. If the universe—and corporations—ran like clocks, then absolute control of the mechanism is not only possible, it is necessary to keep it running efficiently.

On the other side were self-organizing systems theorists who insisted organizations are not "clocks" but living organisms that, once freed of the shackles of control, would naturally learn to organize themselves and flourish. Sides were sharply drawn, and neither wanted to surrender an inch. In its simplest form, the battle seemed to boil down to a monumental disparity in philosophy regarding the fundamental makeup of organizations: Were they objects to be manipulated, or living organisms that would thrive if left alone to adapt at will? Should the focus be on creating a powerful leadership structure or allowing "Whatever happens to happen" or searching for "What is possible here?" Should traditional organizational charts be abandoned in favor of a fluid structure in hopes the organization will self-organize?

Wheatley, in large part, supported the concept that organizations possess the ability to self-organize, provided the conditions are present that allow for self-organization to occur. At the heart of her theory was the idea that organizations could not be understood by using measurements or numbers but rather by studying nature and the rules governing living systems. For her part, Wheatley was not dismissing the importance of measurement. She was only highlighting the limitations inherent when any variable is isolated. Unfortunately, many consultants and others interpreted her words to mean the mechanical side of organizations (measurement, planning, and number crunching, in general) no longer had value.

By the mid-1990s, the self-organizing systems camp, while still highly outnumbered, was attracting a steadily growing number of supporters. We were among those who were intrigued by many of the ideas within the self-organizing systems concept—particularly the idea that people need to participate in the decisions that affect their work. We had always been committed to including the voice of the employee, but the self-organizing systems lens allowed us to add another dimension to our blueprint for creating a thriving organization. In our application of self-organizing systems theory, we learned that the seed of what is possible in organizations can be seen in the living systems of nature—the astonishing synergy between the systems in the human body; the delicate balance between rainfall and a desert blossom; the remarkable interdependence between symbiotic species.

The concepts, ideas, theories, and facts behind self-organizing systems are now widely accepted by the scientific community. However, in the early 1990s, these theories had not yet made great inroads into the corporate world. Wheatley's ideas, coupled with our own research, provided us with a glimpse of what was possible, but we had to be realistic about how the corporate world would embrace this new philosophy. In many cases, corporations refused

to seriously consider the theory of self-organizing systems while they continued to lumber down the ultra-conservative road, fearful of anything too radical. In frustration, sometimes, we wanted to shout at them and say: "You're treating your company and your people like cold, lifeless beings! Don't you understand? They are alive and will adapt and self-organize if allowed to do so!"

We shared the belief of Stuart Kauffman, the scientist who authored *At Home in the Universe: The Search for the Laws of Self-Organization and Complexity*, when he wrote: "The complexity theory is alive. It is concerned with systems that are 'adaptive' and learn from experience the way people do, by evolving and growing in response to changing conditions around them. The complexity theory applies equally to all complex, adaptive systems, whether they are biological cells, a room full of stock traders, or Microsoft Corporation. The critical thing is they are systems."

A few corporate leaders saw promise in the acceptance of self-organizing systems; however, much of the corporate world reacted to the concept with some confusion, and even trepidation. When we proposed a change effort based on self-organizing systems to a company in the United Kingdom, they smiled politely before labeling the proposal as the brainstorm of some "cult." We were not threatened by their reaction; however, this experience, along with many others like it, forced us to acknowledge what our instincts had been telling us all along. Although the premise behind self-organizing systems was sound, for the most part, it was just that—a premise.

Reengineering Versus Self-Organizing Systems

CINDY: But where there is a yin, there also is a yang. The concepts of self-organization and natural evolution left little room for corporate predictability and order, especially on a day-to-day basis. Implementing the premise proved to be a great challenge. For example, while I was working with one of our clients, the Implementation Core Team decided to put one of Meg Wheatley's ideas into practice. In the past, I had always relied upon flip charts to help organize the process; however, Meg stressed that the "self-organizing" process did not require flip charts or, for that matter, discussion notes. "People will act upon decisions without paper," she said.

The employees, managers, and I decided to dispense with the flip charts, as we were tired of using them anyway, and had a wonderful discussion for several hours without recording any of it. In self-organizing systems, meaning is created through conversation, and people are supposed to act accordingly. In reality, we were paralyzed after the meeting because no one could accurately recall what had been said, what commitments had been made, what agreements were reached, and what actions were initiated. The experiment was a disaster. Valuable time was lost in not being able to move forward.

One more story—funny now, but not so funny then—occurred after one customer complained about having been "tossed around" on the company's voice mail system like a "hot potato." Later, when everyone realized no one knew "who" handled that aspect of the business anymore, one person suggested, in jest, that perhaps they should change the message on the company voice mail to indicate: "We're all self-organizing right now. Please call back later." That, and other similar experiments with self-organizing systems, made it clear we had moved too far to the other side of the change continuum.

As trusted consultants, we were not comfortable advising corporate leaders that there was no longer any need for corporate control, internal systems, and measurements or that their company would simply "self-organize" when a problem needed to be solved. Although Wheatley's theories certainly expanded our horizons, we found that scientific theories could easily be skewed when applied to their human equivalent.

Our exposure to self-organizing systems was extremely valuable because it convinced us that organizations, whether they recognized it or not, were closely bound by the laws of nature. The scientific community had validated quantum theories and the impact of delicate system balances in our environment. Consistent with our experiences and everything we believed, organizations were not "equipment" but living organisms without boundaries that are fluid and organic. We were convinced that organizations follow the random, yet "self-organizing" laws of biology and quantum physics more often than they follow the linear, predictable laws of Newton. The majority of corporate leaders today are limited in their effectiveness because they understand only the linear elements of their corporation and fail to grasp the organic aspects. Without a knowledge of the full spectrum, they cannot effectively change, or even sustain, a healthy organization.

We also recognized that viewing organizations solely through the lens of natural law was a flawed perspective. We came to understand the health of a living organization is best understood through an examination of its relational aspects as a "whole" and its traditional, exacting measurements and component parts. One of the reasons for this realization was that Nature has one thing on its side that no organization has—the luxury of geological time. While individual animals must adapt daily to a changing environment, the species itself evolves slowly over hundreds or thousands of years.

Organizations, of course, don't feel they can afford to operate on such a protracted scale of time. Moreover, Nature does not face the same scheduling and regulation restrictions. How many rivers have strict or predictable requirements, like ISO 9000 or current Good Manufacturing Practices (GMPs)? Could Zion National Park in Utah—a geologic wonder because of its natural gifts of wind, rain, and time—have been created on a production schedule with a limited budget? It was obvious the restrictions inherent in the business world placed limits on self-organizing principles that had been so effective in nature.

Our understanding was underscored when Wheatley stated in her subsequent book, *A Simpler Way*, that the self-organizing systems concept is not so much "a call to action" but rather a "meditative call to awareness." Her statement more clearly defined the delineation between us—she is a thinker and theorist of the first order; we are practitioners. While theory and theorists are vital to advances in thinking, we are more focused on practical applications and the ensuing results.

As practitioners of certain aspects of each theory, we appreciate that both sides possess powerful, positive elements. Unfortunately, neither one works by itself! Presented as an either/or choice or dichotomy, neither side represents the whole.

We had previously considered living systems as mutually exclusive concepts to reengineering. In reality, living systems expanded on Newton to include theories he excluded or ignored! What if the concepts of targeted control, measurement, and predictability could work in perfect harmony with the concepts behind self-organizing, living systems? It was not necessary to choose one over the other. In fact, to choose one side, regardless of what it was, would discount at least half of the picture!

The answer lay in a combination of mechanical and living systems that are actually opposite sides of the same coin! However, rather than working together, the two sides typically repel each other like two inverse magnets. As long as they continue to repel rather than attract each other, they will never unite and become a cohesive whole. Therein is the rub! The solution does not fall in either of the opposing camps—but somewhere in the middle!

Eureka! A Solution Emerges

Sometimes ideas and solutions fairly launch themselves into the world with ease and comfort. However, more often than not, they have to simmer and season for a while before they emerge full-blown, hearty, and ready for action. The latter was the case for us in 1993 when we were faced with reconciling the two prevalent organizational views that appeared to be polarized and irreconcilable. Through application with clients and other consultants (the simmer) and researching every piece of literature on corporate and scientific change theories available (the seasoning), the idea—the substance—emerged.

Our challenge became to blend the best ideas, concepts, and practices, regardless of their origin, into an overall approach that actually produced the enduring changes and outcomes that both theorists and practitioners envisioned. For example, aspects of self-organizing systems that ultimately became components of *The Whole Systems Approach* include the Seven Conditions of Thriving Organizations, which came directly from complexity theory. The idea that organizations must be viewed more as living organisms than mechanical beasts is the backbone of our entire approach. The optimum way to change organizations must include both the employee voice and corporate controls. These concepts have become integrated with our own experiences to create our approach.

This approach honors organizations as living systems. But, it also honors profit and mechanical organizational systems. Successful organizations must relentlessly engage in realizing the inherent potential of every person while developing internal systems that ensure high productivity and profitability. To achieve the first goal, everyone—including employees, management, stakeholders, suppliers, and customers—must have a legitimate, accountable voice in how the organization is run. To achieve the second, each of the company's primary systems must be diagnosed, evaluated, and changed wherever necessary.

Throughout our journey of discovery, we were often in the throes of what we term "design chaos." What kept moving us forward was the unwavering belief that in order to achieve our first and primary goal—to unleash the inherent potential residing inside all organizations—our change process had to not only provide employees with a voice in their work, but also develop measurement mechanisms and organizational systems that enabled organizational outcomes to be as predictable and as stable as possible.

By integrating all the available knowledge, we were now ready to develop the concept further—pioneering an approach that worked in the real world. We christened this process *The Whole Systems Approach* because it not only expressed our integrated approach, but it also described our process of involving everyone in changing and running the business.

After 15 years of consulting in organizations and through continual research and development, we articulated the approach in its present form in 1994. The approach is based on an ideal that people can find personal fulfillment while contributing to corporate productivity. Our first-hand experience within organizations has proven *The Whole Systems Approach* can and does apply in the real world! The idea that brought it all together and formed the foundation for *The Whole Systems Approach* was finally distilled into this one simple, but very powerful concept—*organizations are living systems with mechanical parts!*

Section
II

Turning the
Dream into
Reality

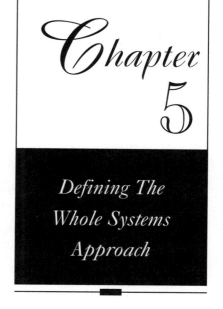

Chapter 5

Defining The Whole Systems Approach

"Liberty means responsibility; that's why people dread it."
—*George Bernard Shaw*

The above quote, attributed to playwright and renowned cynic George Bernard Shaw, is worth noting here because people still use this type of deep cynicism as an excuse not to attempt change. While there may be some people who do dread responsibility, we fail to seek liberty in corporate settings not because we fear or dread it but because we are conditioned to believe it cannot exist there!

We've been programmed to think this way for the last 200 years. Work and drudgery have almost become synonymous terms in many people's minds. How many times have you heard someone say, with excitement in their voice, something like: "Only a few more years, and I can retire! Then I can do what I want!" Or, "Hey, great, it's Wednesday already, hump day."

We faced tremendous barriers while enrolling others in a vision that organizational environments can be changed into exciting, invigorating, and fulfilling communities of people who share a common vision. Moreover, each individual within the community can, in fact, be liberated from their own self-limiting beliefs—realizing their "highest and best self." To make the dream real, our change approach had to be revolutionary—yet grounded in reality.

Even as we were conceiving of a world of work where people and organizations thrived, we recognized the vast difference between concept and reality. We were clear on our goal, but pulling it all together was not so easy. We groped about in the dark much of the time and struggled with constant frustrations. We made mistakes, plenty of them, but managed to keep our vision and our clients intact—a work environment that produced thriving people and outrageous bottom-line results. More than once, we were called "radicals" along the way. But what sustained the storm for us was when people came to understand our dream and bought into it as if it were their own. Invariably, they would be forever changed and would never view the workplace in quite the same way again.

Unleashing Inherent Potential

No organization can reach its potential unless its people are fully vested in—no, make that passionately inspired about—their work. The inspiration comes from a personal alignment with the vision and purpose of the organization and sharing a sense of community at work. The passion comes from having a voice in not only what work we do but how we do our work and in how the organization is run.

The idea of unleashing the latent potential of the company and its employees was extremely compelling. However, we encountered substantial challenges in making the model work. Along with creating a world of work where people thrive, our approach had to increase organizational productivity and provide plenty of clout when it was time to achieve bottom-line figures, sustain the changes over time, ensure the changes were integrated with everything else in the organization, and involve everyone in the process. It was an ambitious goal; yet, thriving people and outrageous results were completely compatible outcomes.

Every study done has confirmed the indisputable—inspired, satisfied employees are more productive than uninspired, dissatisfied ones. Those who look forward to Monday will achieve more than those whose lives "begin" at 5:00 p.m. on Friday. Those who are passionately seeking to realize their inherent potential will, by far, outperform those who are patiently awaiting the 5:00 p.m. whistle. People and corporations with weak self-esteem typically perpetuate low levels of production while those who feel good about their work and themselves cannot be shut down.

Change Triggers

Any one of the following situations can trigger the need for major change. Alignment is key to effectively navigating through turbulent and chaotic times—alignment to an overall strategy and approach consistent with changing and running the business.

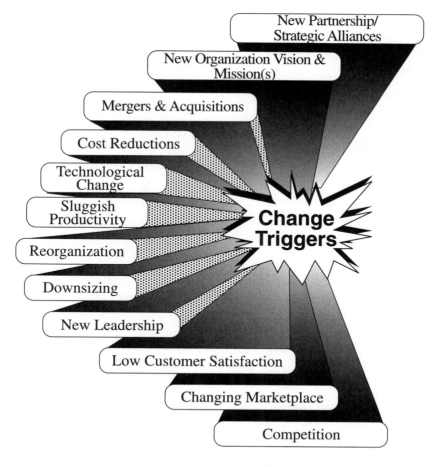

Given the dynamic environment of today's business, change itself must be accomplished quickly within the organization. The pace of life no longer allows for change efforts that last 10 years or more. Even in the past, change efforts of long duration resulted in people becoming impatient with the "snail-like" pace and, in many cases, eventually abandoning the effort. Instead of 10 years, a contemporary effort to change an organization must be complete in less than three years to ensure a competitive advantage in a meaningful timeframe.

The Whole Systems Approach is solidly grounded in practicality. As practitioners, we have learned "what works" and "what can work" inside organizations. This approach is used to both "change and run" the business and is particularly valuable when a need to change fundamentally exists, something is not running effectively or optimally, creating a new possibility will add significant value, or the current effort is not on track—lacking required speed, results, or broad ownership for success.

A Highly Individual and Personal Process

Although this book is about corporate transformation, the truth is transformation is always a highly personal process that depends on individuals. In some instances, people are so profoundly affected by their personal transformation, they tell us, "You gave me back my life" or "I'm a better coach, father, and husband because of what I learned." These statements, and hundreds more like them, reaffirm the value of this approach and the goal of creating a legacy for individuals and organizations.

CINDY: The learning never stops, though sometimes it comes from unexpected sources. For example, my daughter, Aubrie, who is too much like me, wants things to come together right away and is usually "in vision" about possibilities and life. When Bill and I were married, Aubrie was 10 years old. It was the second marriage for both of us. One afternoon, about six months after our wedding, Aubrie was reflecting on what life was like living in two households. She not only had a new brother and sister, she had to maintain two separate bedrooms as she was spending two weeks a month with us and two weeks a month with her father.

One evening, Tyson (my son), Aubrie, and I were out eating dinner. As the conversation continued, she began coaching her brother regarding some concerns he had, and she made a perceptive observation: "I had tried to think it through and work it all out in my head beforehand," she told him. "And I thought I had it all figured out. But, it doesn't work that way. I finally realized that sometimes you just have to live it through."

Her spontaneous comments captured what we had been trying to articulate for years. Learning to "live it through" is a critical step in any change approach. Until we are willing to let go of the notion that we can puzzle out exactly what will happen in the future—and quit fooling ourselves into believing we can control everything—we cannot begin to realize our inherent potential. Leaders must come to understand that organizations do have the ability to "live it through." Sometimes we cannot plan every step, every detail, every aspect of our futures. The truth is the future is a great unknown. We rarely can predict what will happen. Can you even predict with any certainty what will happen during a meeting between two people? How about three people, or ten? Regardless of what some people would like to believe, the future is not predictable.

Does this mean we throw up our hands in despair and do no planning at all? Of course not. What we can do is build a flexible, creative organization that will respond quickly and adapt to unexpected situations and challenges as they arise. Living organisms—trees, birds, fish, animals, and humans—do this on a daily basis. Do you know if someone is going to pull out in front of you on the highway this afternoon? Of course you don't. You don't dwell on the uncertain nature of such a possibility or worry because you are not able to control every vehicle on the highway. Why? Because you feel confident you can take evasive action if needed. We survive in uncertainty every day, and, in fact, thrive on it. We grow stronger because of it. We survive because we can and do adapt. We flourish because we are able to "live it through." Organizations must do the same.

Realizing a Return—Sustaining the Results

This approach can be used to run the business long after the changes are in place, thereby creating sustainable results and organizational self-reliance. This is a significant distinction because once the change effort runs its course, it is often cast aside as an aberration so the company can get "back to normal." This approach represents a process that becomes part of the organization's DNA and balances outstanding business results with valuing people and replicating processes.

A primary reason 80 percent of change efforts fail is they are not designed to be a permanent part of the way the organization does business. As a result, once the change effort is completed and the energy and direction provided by the external consultants are gone, employees often slide back into old habits. This tendency is akin to going on a crash diet rather than making a change in lifestyle.

"I did my job by putting forth the effort required during the change experiment," people often think. "But now I can get back to doing business as usual." Ironically, the change is not seen as part of "doing business." The change effort is viewed as disconnected from their jobs, instead of integral to how they do their jobs. The ideal is obviously a way to change and run the business because change alone is not a long-term solution.

The Whole Systems Approach is a strategy that keeps operating when other change models quit because changing the organization is not enough. Senior leaders must be able to run their organizations using the same principles, philosophies, and strategies used during the change process or their change effort will ultimately fall short of success.

Components of the Whole Systems Approach

This approach is centered on four components, representing different views of the organization:

1. Seven Conditions of Thriving Organizations
Condition-oriented (living; organic; overall health; vital signs)

2. Six Systems of Organizational Effectiveness
Systems-oriented (horizontal; cross-functional mechanisms; interconnectedness)
3. Alignment Model
Alignment-oriented (vertical; general to specific; line-of-sight)
4. Whole System Phases of Transformation
Process-oriented (progressive; sequential; time-bound)

An organic analogy illustrates the relationship of the various components of this approach. The Seven Conditions are the equivalent of sun, water, and nutrients to a growing plant. The Six Systems constitute the garden in which the plants are growing, while the Alignment Model and Phases of Transformation represent the gardener's actions that facilitate healthy growth throughout the garden's life cycle.

Transformation is not a one-time event. Developing the capability for rapid change with a responsible and aligned workforce represents a significant competitive advantage and provides the means to:

- Achieve successful, fundamental change and "corporate reinvention"
- Create a resilient, flexible organization while accelerating the speed of traditional organizational change by a multiple of at least four
- Produce outstanding results that could not have been accomplished using traditional approaches
- Build organizational self-reliance and foster an environment conducive to sustaining a thriving organization and a successful future
- Develop stakeholders who are involved, aligned, and committed to the success of the organization

This approach is designed to leverage the investment in time and resources and contribute to building a cohesive whole. By being persistent (following through) and consistent, an organization can truly transform itself while acquiring the competency to be "change-able."

Applying The Whole Systems Approach in the Real World

One of the primary advantages of this approach is its practicality. Many clients, representing a broad spectrum of industries, have successfully used the entire organization to transform and run their businesses. While we reference a number of those clients in this book, we have chosen to highlight three specific examples that provide a good range of possible applications of *The Whole Systems Approach.*

For example, in one instance, a successful natural gas distribution company used the approach to position the organization for effectively moving from a regulated status to a competitive environment.

In another, an information technology company was faced with a threat to its very survival.

In the third example, a very profitable and highly successful manufacturing company was experiencing rapid growth potential and wanted to expand substantially in the marketplace. They needed to build the infrastructure that would support that growth and secure their market position.

Each of these three case study examples is briefly described here; however, references to specific details of their efforts are used as examples throughout the book.

MichCon: Preparing for Deregulation

In 1989, Michigan Consolidated Gas Company (MichCon) was a 150-year-old gas distribution company headquartered in Detroit. Serving more than 500 communities throughout the state of Michigan, MichCon was the nation's sixth largest local distribution company. By all measures, MichCon had been successful for years. However, Steve Ewing, CEO and president, was concerned that MichCon could not be as competitive as it needed to be in the future. As a fossil-fuel business, the company had been historically heavily regulated. Yet, with deregulation looming on the horizon, Ewing knew he had to prepare his company to thrive when deregulation became a reality.

At the time, MichCon management was top heavy. Activities and functions occurred in a funnel, supervisors had narrow spans of control, and few people below the executive level were empowered to make decisions. Employees were reluctant to assume risks, speak out, or involve themselves. Over the years, employees had become adept at following directions and doing little more than what they were instructed to do.

As Ewing observed, "We had mastered all the tools available to us and knew the next level of performance had to come from within via individual contribution. People would hold the key to reaching that next level. We wanted to focus on increasing employee satisfaction and performance while keeping the customer at the center of our universe. One conventional way to reorganize a company is to lock the vice presidents in a room and 'just do it.' We'd used that approach in the past. This time, however, we opted for an approach that would engage the entire organization."

In January 1990, MichCon kicked off a high-involvement process (still in place today) to continually reposition itself as the "premier" organization in its industry based on the perception of its 1.2 million customers. MichCon's evolution has been based on a commitment to continually reinvest in its employees to ensure everyone recognizes the opportunity inherent in deregulation and willingly aligns to a shared vision, common values, and a focus on the customer.

To help accomplish its objectives, MichCon opted to conduct a series of large group conferences. Over five months, approximately 300 employees, representing all levels of the organization, participated in each conference with 10 percent of participants as repeats to ensure continuity from one conference to the next. During each conference, the rest of the organization's members were updated daily via MCTV (the in-house TV channel) and news releases.

When each conference was completed, participants assumed the responsibility to carry key messages back to the organization; then, all employees helped create the necessary input for the next conference. In this way, the entire company actively participated in the conferences and had a legitimate voice in the agreed-upon decisions, whether people were actually "in the room" or not.

In 1999, MichCon continues to perform as one of the most profitable U.S. utilities. MichCon's Operations and Maintenance budget is significantly less than when the effort was launched—proof that employees are working more effectively than in the past. The employee population has dropped from a high of 4,200 to 2,800, all through natural attrition, while MichCon has been attracting new customers at a rate of 20,000 per year. The company has earned its highest-ever customer satisfaction rating at 100 percent in five work groups and an average of 92 percent in the others, all of which Ewing attributes to the foundation established to help his company transform itself ahead of its time.

Clearly, the effort at MichCon would not have been as successful if Ewing had been an episodic leader and activity-driven. Given Ewing's admitted impatience, his demonstrated commitment to the long term and involving everyone in the organization was an anchor for others. "We've tried a lot of things, some of which worked, some of which didn't," Ewing revealed to an audience of utility executives in February 1997. "Some yielded excellent results. Some left lots of room for improvement. However, from my perspective, the single most significant accomplishment was the changing of the company's course and basing the fundamentals of its guidance system on the shift from regulation to competition."

First Security Information Technology: Do or Die!

When Maxcomm entered First Security Information Technology, Inc., much of the "set the stage" or preliminary work on their change effort had already been accomplished with the support of another consultant who had been helping them lay the groundwork for almost a year. At the time, the effort was stalled and needed broader organizational member involvement and ownership. The leader described the circumstances as, "We broke our pick on this one; we needed a new tool." Maxcomm was invited to partner with the company's consultant in completing the effort.

As the leadership team began to establish the parameters for the effort, they agreed the change needed to be radical and had to involve the whole system. They elected to sponsor a series of four large group conferences during the whole systems change process. The conferences were so productive, the organization continued to use conferencing technology throughout the implementation phase and adopted it as a standard methodology for running the business.

The initial large group conference created momentum with all the employees around the Business Imperative for Change: "Our parent company needs technology to be successful. We are failing our parent company. Radical change is required for us to survive and succeed." From this point, the company initiated massive, radical change in process, structure, and human competencies. In the space of 18 months, this company shifted from one on the verge of extinction to a recognized leader in the financial industry as deemed by their greatest critic, the parent company. Additionally, at the beginning of the effort, they had never experienced one "flawless service delivery day." Today, flawless delivery days have become the norm rather than the exception.

"When you compare the yearly performance of our flawless processing in relation to the threshold, we're not where we want to be yet," noted Verlin Mortensen of the Quality Improvement Team on Flawless Daily Processing, "but that doesn't tell the whole story. If we think in terms of continuous improvement, we have to look at the trends. When we do that, the data show we have made a lot of progress over a very short time, and we're definitely headed in the right direction."

GOJO: Capitalizing on the Opportunity for Growth

GOJO Industries, Inc., an Akron-based professional skin care company, began as an entrepreneurial company over 50 years ago. This privately held, mid-sized company was co-founded by a husband-and-wife team. GOJO manufactures and markets hand hygiene and skin care products in 50 countries. Over the years, GOJO has steadily grown.

The company leaders understood that if they continued to grow, they would lose their ability to react to the marketplace quickly, their agility, their entrepreneurial attitude, and their sense of family—all of which had contributed to their success. They also knew they needed to grow. Their opportunities were promising, and deeper market penetration was essential in their very competitive environment of manufacturing and distribution.

In order to accomplish the anticipated growth, they had to create an open system with the needed infrastructure that would preserve their entrepreneurial spirit and agility but would also increase their quality and help them comply with GMP requirements. They decided to create an organization that was ever learning, changeable, and a "thriving leader in professional skin care."

This was no small task. They kicked off *The Whole Systems Approach* in 1995 and held their celebration to mark the end of the change and transition phases in January 1998. During that time, they reinvented themselves from every possible angle. They engaged the organization in a series of four large group conferences and are now using this stakeholder involvement technique as a natural part of the way they do business, even to the point of using it in schools with kids to teach children about the importance of hand hygiene for good health.

Their results have been significant since they initiated the transformation journey:

- Sustained double-digit growth
- Substantially increased profitability
- Reengineered or introduced several key processes
- Launched a new business venture by seizing a "first to market" opportunity and creating the consumer instant hand sanitizer category with the launch of Purell® brand Instant Hand Sanitizer.

Total Participation and Integration

Embedding a system for total employee participation is crucial. The high-level involvement strategy that is fundamental to this approach is intended to result in employee "buy-in" of purpose, vision, and values, with commitment to collective and personal responsibility. Bound by a shared vision and freed from rigid job descriptions, each employee can be developed and nurtured to become effective in a more decentralized, dynamic structure.

Any change approach, however, cannot end with just the employees. It has to be a completely integrated effort involving the entire system, from stakeholders and suppliers to management and customers. This full integration helps build a strong sense of organizational community and identity. And, it does not stop with the people component. It also weaves the systems, templates, tools, practices, and common language into the organizational fabric. At the same time, it challenges every person involved within the organization.

The Whole Systems Approach should carry a notice on the label: WARNING! THIS APPROACH SHOULD NOT BE USED BY THE MEEK AND MILD!

This approach is not about changing who is in charge of the paper clips. It is about Change with a capital "C." *The Whole Systems Approach* is one of the most comprehensive efforts any organization can undertake. The paradigm shift that occurs with nearly every employee, stakeholder, vendor, and customer is profound. As a leader, be forewarned that once you begin this process, you can never turn back. The loss in reputation is too high. Of course, you will never want to turn back. We promise that those who embark on this odyssey of discovery and improvement will never view their work again through the same lenses.

Last summer, we planted portulaca, a desert plant, in our front flower bed. This particular flower bed had soil that was nutrient rich, moist, and was partially shaded during the morning hours. We knew this flower bed was not the best place for this particular plant; however, we loved the look of the plant and wanted it in front of our home.

At first, the portulaca thrived. It grew so well, we teased each other about it being on steroids. We marveled at this lush, thick plant with large, beautiful, bright flowers covering the entire flower bed. "We have defied nature," we said to each other. "This plant likes it here!"

Chapter 6

Diagnosing Organizational Health: Seven Conditions of Thriving Organizations

Unfortunately, our euphoria was short-lived, and we were faced with a dose of reality. Like a plant that had been on a "bad trip," overnight the portulaca zapped out, suffered a nervous breakdown, and literally withered away. Although the portulaca had put on a magnificent show for us in our "rich conditions," it was a desert plant that needed dry soil, little water, and full sun to thrive over the long term. It was not able to remain healthy given the conditions we had provided for it.

Organizations are no different. In order for people and the organization to thrive long term and ensure they do not suffer a "steroid bust" like the one our portulaca experienced, careful attention must be placed on the conditions that ensure health. This, of course, begs the questions "What constitutes health in an organization?" and "How healthy is your organization overall?" At first, these may seem like easy questions. However, the more we consider the answers, the more elusive they become. Most people struggle to find anything more definitive than generalities such as, "Well, our health is good. We're doing some positive things." or "It could be better." Others point to profit margins and quarterly earnings for an answer.

It doesn't take long for the point of this question to become clear. Despite its overriding importance, many people have difficulty defining organizational health. Most are not sure what constitutes good organizational health, let alone how to measure it within their organizations. The way an organization chooses to take its own pulse often reveals as much about the organization's state of health as does the pulse rate itself!

The dilemma of diagnosing organizational health stems from the "organization-as-machine" paradigm. Those who still insist organizations are lifeless entities often find they cannot understand the question at all. If an organization is viewed as a sterile object, mechanical in design and nature, the concept of organizational health has no relevance.

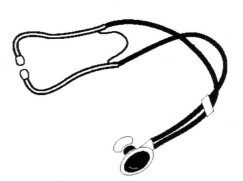

How can you take the pulse of a machine?

On the other hand, if we view organizations as entities that live, breathe, form, and reform in response to the environment, an enormous philosophical and practical shift occurs. Once this transpires, ensuring vigor and robust health will emerge as a constant and critical concern. Living things are either healthy or unhealthy. Healthy organisms thrive and grow. Unhealthy ones flounder and, eventually, die.

No organism can sustain high levels of performance without being fit. In today's fluid marketplace, organizations must be as superbly conditioned as any top professional athlete, or they risk being left behind in someone else's dust. This is true for all living things: the more competitive the environment, the more critical good health is to survival. That is why learning to recognize and maintain the health of the organization is so important.

Thriving, living organizations share a set of common conditions that affect their health. These conditions are much like the vital organs within a human body. They must be understood and nurtured for the organization to perform at optimal levels. The identification of these Seven Conditions evolved out of work with diverse companies including utilities, banking, manufacturing, healthcare, hospitality, and high technology. Although each organization differed widely in terms of outlook, purpose, size and structure, they shared similarities. These companies are like human beings who come in a variety of shapes, sizes, and colors. We may be unique on the outside, but we all share common internal organs such as a brain, lungs, heart, liver, and kidneys. These must all remain healthy for us to reach our peak performance levels.

Organizations are no different. Regardless of size, style, function, or geographical location, they share similar internal conditions. These distinct conditions exist in every company and are crucial to the overall health of the organization. The process of discovering the Seven Conditions allowed us to develop repeatable diagnostic and improvement procedures to assess and address each condition.

One of the emerging roles of leaders is to become an organizational doctor who can effectively diagnose and maintain the health of these Seven Conditions:

1. *Information:* the lifeblood that flows through and nourishes the entire organization
2. *Participation:* the key factor in the organization's potential for limitless possibilities
3. *Relationships:* the context for results within the organization
4. *Adaptability:* the ability to respond to changing conditions

5. *Creativity:* the renewal capacity for infusing the system with new energy and results
6. *Interconnectedness:* the threads that comprise the fabric of interdependence throughout the organization
7. *Identity:* the DNA that connects the organization's past and future in the present

When physicians begin complete checkups on patients, they focus on the patients' vital signs. The Seven Conditions constitute the vital signs of a living organization. When these conditions do not exist or are weak, the organization can become diseased and sluggish.

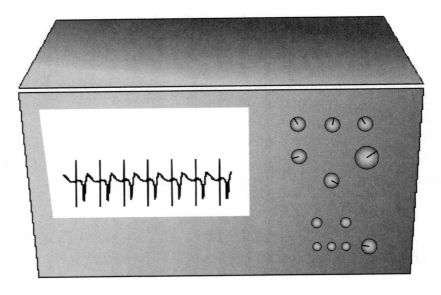

Becoming qualified to evaluate your own company's health is much like completing a course in "organizational medicine." Your first challenge as an "organizational intern" is to familiarize yourself with the characteristics of each condition and the symptoms that indicate when that condition may be at risk of disease. After reviewing each condition, use the self-assessment guides provided at the end of this chapter to check the vital signs and diagnose the current state of that condition within your own organization.

1. Information: Organizational Lifeblood

Information is the source of all transformation. All healthy systems openly exchange information within their own environments and with the outside world. Every day we have access to information that has the potential to transform us. This information is a gift we can choose to integrate, deny, or ignore. The brain is constantly processing the information received through the body's sensors. Responses to that information help the individual move, eat, think, and act. By the same token, an organization must continually process information to respond appropriately to the market, customers, and needs of the organization itself.

Information is the lifeblood of the entire system. Like the circulation system, it is critical to organizational health. Restrict it in any way, and disease results. The channels through which information passes are mechanical, similar to the branching veins and arteries that stretch out for miles throughout the body. New data, like oxygenated blood, is organic and life-giving. When information is plentiful, it flows through the company, nourishing and rejuvenating the entire system. Outdated information, like carbon dioxide, needs to be purged. To stay ahead of the competition, capitalize on available input, and effectively act on feedback, organizations must develop a healthy respect for and valuing of information—data regard. Unfortunately, many organizations unconsciously embrace the opposite philosophy—data disregard.

One of the most tragic examples of data disregard—a common breakdown in organizational information systems—exploded before our eyes on television screens on January 28, 1986. The space shuttle, Challenger, once America's spectacular technological achievement and symbol of hope for the future, soared brilliantly across the cold morning sky. Then, as millions of people watched in horror, the shuttle suddenly veered, burst into flames, and corkscrewed downward, carrying seven people to their deaths.

The intensive investigation that followed placed most of the technical blame for the shuttle's failure on the rubber O-rings sealing the four main segments of the 116-foot-long solid fuel rocket motor. The O-rings were stiff and slow to respond to the morning's freezing temperatures. However, the real blame can ultimately be attributed to data disregard. Prior to the launch, engineers warned shuttle managers that the O-rings might malfunction in the cold. A launch delay was recommended, but under the vise-like pressures of schedule and cost, NASA managers made a fatal decision. They disregarded the warning and ordered the launch. One manager later admitted the information that could have averted the disaster was available. "But, an amnesia epidemic broke out that obscured any memory of those communications," he said.

Challenger is a graphic example of why it is crucial that all employees not only have access to the information they need but are also encouraged to make appropriate decisions on what to do with that information. The success of any business depends largely on the free exchange of information. It is as essential for an organization as it is for a physical body to live, breathe, and grow.

A recurring problem within organizations is the hoarding of information by employees and leaders who use it as a control mechanism or political currency. This petty power-brokering slows the company's internal processes. Unchecked, it can cause a breakdown of the entire system.

Not long ago, we observed a graphic example of such a breakdown. One of our clients received a bomb threat phoned in by an unidentified caller. The caller said the bomb was on the manufacturing floor at the company's headquarters. Senior leaders immediately caucused and outlined a battle plan to deal with the emergency. Unfortunately, they had difficulty communicating their message to the organization as they had never established a formal company-wide communication system. As a result, important information went out to the 500 employees in a piecemeal fashion. A variety of rumors were started because of the scattered way in which the information moved from unit to unit and division to division. But the ultimate thrust of this interaction was that management did not take the bomb threat seriously. To make matters worse, employees were told they could evacuate; however, they would not be compensated for their time off the line. The message communicated was, "We don't think the bomb threat is real, but if you see a strange package, don't touch it. Call us."

This incident occurred during the day shift, and the company had no way of relaying the information about the bomb threat to those on the other two shifts. The night shift learned of the threat through the grapevine, and rumors spread like wildfire. The story became more exaggerated with each iteration. For nearly a month afterwards, dozens of wild rumors persisted throughout the organization regarding the nature of the threat.

Employee response was predictable. Many were furious at management's mishandling of the situation. They felt the company did not care about them. Some quit their jobs outright, while others quit in every way, except officially. In the long run, no bomb was ever found in the building except the one that went off in the hearts of the employees!

In the months following this incident, we were asked to help settle the fallout from the situation. The first thing we did was establish an organization-wide communication system, which was fully tested six months later when a company employee died suddenly of an unusual virus. The employee had often handled toxic materials on the manufacturing floor, making his death a potential source of frightening rumors. To nip these rumors in the bud, management utilized the new communication channel to immediately notify the entire company about the employee's death. The company then brought in local health officials to explain how the employee had succumbed to a non-contagious disease. Management and the local health officials reassured employees that the death had nothing to do with the work environment.

The company then went a step further. Grief counselors were brought in, and employees were encouraged to consult with the counselors. The CEO also established a fund for the employee's family. Employees were given time off to attend the funeral. It was the right and decent reaction to the tragedy, and it solidified trust within the organization. People felt an added sense of community within the company. Unlike the bomb threat fiasco, management made it clear they valued employees as people.

2. Participation: Tapping Inherent Potential

What would it mean to your company if you could tap into 100 percent of the potential of every employee? Most corporate leaders estimate only a small portion of their organization's potential is being realized. In some cases, the estimates are downright dismal. The administrators of a prestigious university once estimated that as little as 15 percent of the staff's human potential was being exercised. They could only wonder how effective the university could be if this latent potential could be tapped.

In the past 20 years, concepts such as Quality Circles, empowerment, self-directed work teams, and total quality management (TQM) have made much of employee participation within organizations. What most leaders have failed to realize is that "open-door" policies are not enough. Tapping potential and full participation are tightly linked.

One question that every employee who works within a living organization should ask is, "Who makes the decisions that affect my work?" When the answer is, "You make most of the decisions that affect your work," then employees are far more likely to buy into the company's values and vision.

We once worked with senior leaders from a major software development company in the healthcare industry. They told us with pride that they had just completed a corporate-wide TQM effort to solicit suggestions and recommendations from their employees. We thought this commendable until we talked with the employees, who scoffed when we brought up the subject, indicating it was the sixth time in three years they had been asked the same questions. None of the employee recommendations had ever been implemented. One employee said it reminded him of the *Peanuts* comic strip where Lucy promises to hold the football so Charlie Brown can kick it. At the last moment, she jerks it away, and Charlie Brown inevitably winds up flat on his back.

PEANUTS reprinted by permission of United Feature Syndicate, Inc.

"We're just like Charlie Brown," the employee lamented. "The company keeps saying to us, 'Come on, just one more time. Trust us.'"

In this company, though, as in many others, Charlie Brown wised up. Some employees eventually left the company while many just quit trying. Senior leaders were confronted with a increasingly hostile and cynical workforce, resulting in a crisis that seriously damaged the company's productivity.

To gain perspective, senior leaders must ask themselves: "Who don't you want to participate?" A hypothetical question, of course, because the reality is everyone in the organization participates in one way or another—if not in a positive way, then in a negative one. A typical story we hear repeated in corporation after corporation involves employees who wanted to contribute some valuable ideas during a meeting but weren't invited to attend. Feeling dissatisfied, the employees consumed considerable time and energy expressing their anger and resentment to those around them.

Like it or not, every person in your organization is already participating, either by putting energy into the system or by taking it
out. Whenever there is less than 100 percent participation, energy
that would otherwise go toward creating goods or providing services
is lost. Often, this is a hidden, but insipid, energy drain. It slowly
weakens the organization by limiting positive possibilities for new
ways of working, results, and energized employees. Over time, or in
the event the marketplace becomes highly competitive, such weak-
ness can prove fatal.

Of course, along with participation comes responsibility. This is
not Utopia. Within almost all organizations, there will be what we
term the "glazed donuts"—people who sit with a glazed look, waiting to be told what to do. Not everyone will want to participate and
shoulder the attendant responsibility. But, in unleashing the inherent potential among those who do, encouraging participation will
infuse your organization with a powerful new energy.

3. Relationships: The Context for Results

What type of relationships exist within your organization? Are
they built upon mutual trust and respect? Are employees free to
build collaborative relationships with whomever they need to so
they can do their work? During crises, do these relationships pull
people together or push them apart? Do employees nurture each
other's inherent potential and build community or does political
gamesmanship dominate?

It is critical that leaders address these questions because relationships form the new context through which work is accomplished and products or services are rendered.

We are moving toward relationship-based organizations where
chains of command and top-down authority are less important.
Influence within the living organization is created through quality
relationships, or not at all. As much time as needed must be invested into developing these relationships.

Bob Solum, in whose wonderful memory we've dedicated this
book, was a terrific relationship builder. As a consultant to a variety

of domestic organizations, he inspired trust and inspiration in others because he believed a good relationship brought him freedom. He felt it gave him the liberty to move quickly because he knew he could call on people when he needed help. In return, he was always available for anyone who needed him.

Even after his premature death, we continue to learn from Bob. Of the more than 200 people who attended his funeral, nearly every person felt they had been Bob's best friend. It was a sincere, authentic feeling spanning all age groups. One of Bob's neighbors, a tough, 75-year-old ex-Marine, wept openly. He told us that despite the impossible work schedule Bob maintained, he always made time to share a cup of coffee and warm conversation. A 16-year-old daughter of one of Bob's friends told us: "He listened to me. Most adults don't. I felt like somebody special around him."

Sometimes it's easy to feel that business relationships are nothing more than obligatory, time-consuming burdens. Bob never saw them like that. He saw relationships as something that fed and nourished him. He gladly invested the energy to maintain these relationships, often long after the connection to business had lapsed. He was convinced relationships make everything work. It is the quality of those relationships that allow us to be who we are. He liked to ask two questions that seemed to sum it all up: "What relationships have you maintained and enhanced in your lifetime?" and "If it's not about that, what else is it about?" Bob clearly understood what was important in business and in life.

From a professional standpoint, the quality of relationships can make a significant difference in the health of the company. Not long ago, we witnessed the CEOs of two multinational companies call off a $120 million deal because they could not get along. Both companies had a tremendous amount to gain through the partnership; however, neither man trusted the other. Part of the problem was they never really talked to each other. In a way, these two men mirrored the way many corporations operate today. We are always amazed at how often people within a single organization have never even met each other, let alone developed a working relationship.

The only reason the situation changed between these two companies was that one of the men retired. Luckily, the CEO who replaced him understood what a potential alliance could mean, and he arranged a face-to-face meeting with the other CEO. They found they shared much common ground and a deal was struck. They now exchange more than $300 million in business between them. It has been a tremendous benefit to both companies. But, because of a poor relationship, it took seven years and a change of leadership for the deal to work.

Human beings are social animals. We have an inherent need for relationships. The better these are, the more productive and satisfied we are. Leaders should always keep that fact in mind. The better the relationships within a team, the better the results that team will produce. The quality of the relationships within your organization will do much to determine its success or failure. It is not only important but enlightening to consider how many people within your organization have a positive relationship with each other. The greater the number, the healthier your organization will be.

4. Adaptability: The Ability to Respond

Organizations must continually adapt to meet changing global market demands. One leader expressed adaptability in this way: "It is sort of like taking off from New York with a DC3 and landing in Chicago with a Concorde and never interrupting the meal service along the way."

The ability to change quickly to meet new customer and market requirements is continually increasing in importance. Employees and management must be prepared to adapt their way of doing work almost daily. Newfangled hardware is not enough. In one utility company that owned every high-tech gadget on the market, leadership was troubled. The company was not moving nearly as fast or efficiently as they had hoped it would.

When they asked us to intervene, we found that while the company had all the technological bells and whistles, the outlook of most employees was woefully outdated. Employees were still grousing about changes made by senior management more than 10 years before! They hated and feared change. They felt it was always something that was done to them, not for them. The more the senior leaders tried to change the company, the more the employees resisted. On the outside, the organization appeared to be a future-oriented company, ready to take on all challengers. However, on the inside, it had the flexibility of an iron post and a very questionable future.

In another example, WordPerfect, in its "heyday," invested 10 months on a major release only to have its marketing department declare the product outdated. The work team took a collective deep breath, adapted to the change, never missed a beat, and went back to work redesigning the product. Within a few months, the company had the new release ready to ship. Positive management and employee attitudes are not enough, though. Internal systems must be in place to allow for the necessary flexibility. The structure must be functional, and employees and work teams must be willing to act and assume responsibility for their actions.

Like any living organism, organizations must constantly adapt to their environment. Change must be understood as a natural process that is both embraced and resisted. The human body regenerates and changes constantly. As spring always follows winter, change and renewal within organizations are natural events. It is essential organizations view change as a partner to creativity and productivity rather than as an enemy. It is essential that the condition of adaptability be so fine-tuned that organization members are able to "re-spond" versus being in the position to only "re-act" to changing situations and circumstances.

5. Creativity: The Capacity for Renewal

Creativity is essential for building momentum and renewing capacity within the organization. Any organization not creating is falling behind. As human beings, we share a fundamental need to contribute through the creation of new products, services, systems, or programs. When creativity is allowed to thrive within the organization, new possibilities emerge. These possibilities promote changes that invigorate the environment, stimulate growth, and develop the capacity for renewal.

The cycles and seasons in nature have their own form of creativity. We notice the emergence of flowers in the spring, when dormant plants are stimulated to grow to their full development, enhancing the environment with scents, forms, and colors. But there is also creativity in the residual months of autumn, such as when a tree loses its leaves. Even in its state of decline, the tree is still creating protection for the grass and foliage below with layers of insulation against harsh winter temperatures. Each stimulus and response in the natural world is constantly producing or laying the "groundwork" for another form of life to emerge and take its place.

Organizations must not only be able to adapt, they must be able to constantly create, or they run the risk of suffering from poor results and low organizational self-esteem. Individuals within the organization may receive fulfillment in different ways—enhancing, modifying, innovating, or otherwise affecting a product or service. Regardless of the means, individuals can consequently appreciate the vital role they play in the creation of new products or services.

To be effective, of course, creation must be paired with action and completion. Together, creation and completion build upon the essential rhythms of the company involving idea-building, growth, and the natural energy and optimism that spring from growth.

6. Interconnectedness: The Fabric of Interdependence

The human body is the epitome of a system that exhibits order, cooperation, and interdependency. It is synergistic in nature and subject to natural laws. Each organ has its unique function, just as each cell has its own blueprint. The body's organs, limbs, and cells contribute to the whole. If the heart is weak, we don't cut off the legs so the heart doesn't have to work so hard. The same is true of business organizations. If profits are sagging, slashing the workforce will not ensure profits will rise. If the cause of the profit slump is some type of defective or inefficient process, laying off many employees will not improve product quality. To resolve the problem and ensure organizational health, management must move from a reactive mode to a proactive one; from thinking of organizations as machines to thinking of them as living systems.

To demonstrate the condition of interconnectedness, we often hand out balls of yarn to employees who participate in one of our sessions. We ask the participants to hold the string in one hand while tossing the rest of the ball to someone on whom they depend to do their work. That person, in turn, holds onto the string and tosses the ball to someone else. After a short time, people are surprised to see that the yarn connects most people and crisscrosses the room to create a web.

After this exercise, people understand that what they do clearly affects others. But connectivity doesn't stop there. It is equally important for everyone in the organization to gain a clear perspective of the organization's place within the local and global marketplaces. No company can operate in a vacuum. Everyone within the organization must be clear on how their work affects customers, other employees, and stakeholders.

A few years ago, we met with a group of service people working in a large metropolitan hotel that was part of a worldwide chain. During our work with the hotel, we heard from a manager who was frustrated that a project he had in mind had been "shot down" for no apparent reason. While searching for ways to increase the hotel's revenue, he discovered the hotel's laundry facilities were not being used to capacity. He found a client willing to pay $300,000 a year for laundry services the hotel could easily provide without sacrificing or compromising its own needs. The manager, believing he had just uncovered a financial bonanza for the company, was shocked when his request to begin operations was denied.

It was not until all the parties involved sat down together that the story began to unfold. What our progressive-minded manager did not know was that the operation required another department manager to ask a few of his employees to work overtime. A short time before, that manager had been given orders to reduce overtime in his department, so he naturally refused the request. The overtime would have amounted to about $14,000 a year. Once these two managers talked and understood the entire situation, they quickly approved the overtime expenditure. Until they understood how they were connected, these managers were unable to see their way clear to bringing in $300,000 of highly profitable business.

In most organizations few people have a clear understanding of how they are all connected. When the right hand does not know what the left hand is doing, many opportunities are missed.

7. Identity: Corporate DNA

Although many leaders attempt to design a plan for change, they often do not consider the organization's culture. All living things have a genetic code; organizations are no exception. The genetic code—corporate DNA—is the context that produces all outcomes for the company: both positive and negative. It provides the building blocks of meaning. The culture actually controls what, how, and when tasks are done. It is very difficult to change the core culture. All work, relationships, and interactions are governed by norms that become part of the corporate genetics and are maintained within the system.

Every person in the organization needs a sense of organizational history and a clear understanding of the organization's direction for the future. This vision, sense of purpose, and organizational identity are sometimes the only things to which employees and leaders can cling during times of chaos and crisis. The Biblical adage "Without vision, people perish" is particularly relevant to our contemporary organizations.

GOJO Industries recently helped solidify its organizational identity by connecting with its customers. GOJO established the purpose statement: "Well-being through handwashing and healthy skin." Going a step further, the company surveyed a number of auto mechanics who used a GOJO product called HAND MEDIC™ Antiseptic Skin Treatment. GOJO shared the responses with their employees.

"My hands have been cracked and sore for 20 years," one mechanic said. "Your product made it possible for me to go through a day without pain. The quality of my life is better." Another HAND MEDIC user reported, "This is the first time in years I've been able to touch family members without it discomforting them. It has improved our relationship."

Reading and hearing about these responses allowed employees—whether they were on the manufacturing floor, in sales, R&D, or elsewhere—to feel pride in their work and appreciate how they were part of an effort that improved people's lives. This knowledge elevated the employees above the everyday work and gave them a higher purpose and shared identity. Without a shared identity, there can be no creation of corporate memory or sense of organizational soul and spirit.

Shared identity comes through coloring in the past, honoring it, and also tracing in the lines of the future, such that we are more fully able to act with assurance, a real knowing of who we are in the present. Shared identity is the foundation for corporate meaning. Identity is "who we are," our image and reputation.

One company we worked with had lost their identity without an awareness they had even done so. The company started out as a "mom and pop" shop headquartered in the founders' garage. Operating on a shoestring, they could not afford to pay high wages, but they compensated by creating a sense of family and encouraging camaraderie. Many years later as the company grew and was highly profitable, the company continued to pay low wages while eliminating references to "family" from all the corporate memos. In the process, the enterprise lost the esprit de corps it had once enjoyed. Morale plummeted, and the workforce became disconnected, to say the least.

Later, during a large group gathering, the employees and leaders were reconnected to the company's history and discovered the reason why they were so dissatisfied. They had lost the sense of family and camaraderie. That very day, a feeling of family was reintroduced into the company. Spirit and family have become part of their core identity—the recognized DNA essential for the company to carry forward.

Purpose is why the organization exists. Vision is what we declare to create and serves as a compelling future to which we can all align. Values are the day-to-day guidelines by which organizational members choose to live. Together, they form the organization's identity. Unfortunately, in the last 10 years, so much jargon has been coined around purpose, vision, and values that these elements—so crucial to the definition of the organization and essential to employee loyalty—have been trivialized. In a fulfilling organization, the purpose of most individual members aligns with the stated purpose of the organization. When such alignment occurs, people typically find passion in their work. The alignment of individual and organizational purpose generates excitement, stimulates creativity, contributes to quality relationships, and affects outstanding bottom-line productivity.

Fulfillment and maximum productivity are achieved only in an environment where each member has an opportunity to grow, makes a meaningful contribution, and enjoys a sense of individual and collective purpose.

Maintaining Organizational Health

Many organizations do not realize their potential because they do not involve the whole system and focus too much on short-term results. Unfortunately, many leaders feel that once the blueprint is in place, the implementation and long-term objectives have also been accomplished. The resources, time, and money are then diverted to other things, and the change cannot be sustained. The systems and practices used during the change process do not have a chance to penetrate the culture. The need to "declare victory and move on" is the Achilles' heel of nearly all change efforts.

To avoid this trap, a clearly defined, ongoing set of expectations, along with a methodology for reaching them, needs to be embedded in the organization. That's exactly what the Seven Conditions provide. Change and improvement begin with awareness. If the Seven Conditions can be kept in a state of vitality and robust health, the company will not only succeed during the change effort, but also thrive over the long run. The Seven Conditions serve as the bridge, linking the changing of the business with the running of it.

Seven Conditions Informal Assessments

After completing each of the assessment guides that follow, you should have a sense of the state of your company's vital signs; however, an abstract understanding of organizational health isn't enough. The concept has to be translated into everyday practices and behaviors. Otherwise, it's like owning the fastest jet in the world without access to any supplies of jet fuel. It's a great conversation piece, but it won't get you anywhere.

So, evaluate your organization or team on each of the Seven Conditions of Thriving Organizations using the following guides. Answer each question on a scale of 0 to 100 percent with 100 being the ideal. Anything less than 70 percent indicates a need for corrective action. A score below 50 percent indicates an *urgent* need for action.

Information Self-Assessment

Question	Rating
1. What percentage of the employees and leaders in your organization can be provided critical information at a moment's notice utilizing your formal communication system?	
2. What percentage of your managers and senior leaders provide information freely to their direct reports?	
3. What percentage of the employees trust the information provided by management through the communication system?	
4. What percentage of your organization's employees understand the strategic direction of your company?	
5. What percentage of the employees know how the organization is currently doing from a business standpoint?	
6. What percentage of the employees know how their team or unit contributes to the achievement of business results?	
7. When vital information is exchanged, how often is it done face-to-face, as opposed to memos, letters, and voicemail?	
AVERAGE SCORE (Total of Rating divided by 7)	

Participation Self-Assessment

Question	Rating
1. During meetings, what percentage of employees and managers provide suggestions and ideas to better your internal systems?	
2. What percentage refuse to participate for fear of looking bad or being evaluated?	
3. How many employees regularly participate in defining and improving how their work gets done?	
4. What percentage are asked to help establish performance standards?	
5. What percentage of the total potential of the people within your organization are you accessing?	
6. What percentage of people are asked for feedback on strategic direction, cultural values, and systems improvements?	
AVERAGE SCORE (Total of Rating divided by 6)	

Relationships Self-Assessment

Question	Rating
1. What percentage of employees seek out and develop relationships within the company necessary to accomplish their work?	
2. What percentage of your people are willing to rely on each other to get work done?	
3. How often do you celebrate together?	
4. What percentage of people are willing to constructively make suggestions and help others when necessary?	
5. What percentage of your managers and senior leaders from different parts of the organization talk to each other regularly?	
6. What percentage of your organization trusts and respects one another?	
AVERAGE SCORE (Total of Rating divided by 6)	

Adaptability Self-Assessment

Question	Rating
1. What percentage of the time do the results of customer interactions lead to modifications in your business procedures?	
2. What percentages of the work processes and systems in your organizations have been changed and improved in the past 12 months?	
3. What percentage of your managers or leaders consistently implement new methods for doing the work more efficiently?	
4. What percentage of employees are coached and challenged to operate outside their "comfort zones"?	
5. What percentage of your people are more eager to make positive changes in work processes than to argue against the changes?	
AVERAGE SCORE (Total of Rating divided by 5)	

Creativity Self-Assessment

Question	Rating
1. What percentage of the organization utilizes an established process for sharing new learning and discoveries at work?	
2. What percentage of the organization recognizes it is necessary and beneficial to periodically redesign their work?	
3. What percentage of the organization is exposed to outside experiences with customers and vendors and utilizes these experiences to improve their work processes?	
4. What percentage of employees consistently challenge existing practices and procedures in an effort to make them better?	
5. How often does your organization seek new ways to fully utilize employee talents and skills?	
6. What percentage of employees are confident in the organization's ability to create <u>new</u> products and services?	
AVERAGE SCORE (Total of Rating divided by 6)	

Interconnectedness Self-Assessment

Question	Rating
1. What percentage of the people within your organization share common long-range goals and objectives?	
2. What percentages of people clearly understand how their actions affect the work of other employees?	
3. What percentage of people see a connection with the customer, no matter how far removed they are?	
4. What percentage of people are encouraged to seek feedback from others about how they do their jobs?	
5. What percentage of the organization's measures of performance are closely tied to the company's strategic goals?	
AVERAGE SCORE (Total of Rating divided by 5)	

Identity Self-Assessment

Question	Rating
1. What percentage of people in your organization know how and why the company was founded?	
2. What percentage of people know how their contribution relates to the purpose and vision of the business?	
3. What percentage of the leaders clearly exemplify the organization's vision and values?	
4. What percentage of people have personal goals that align with those of the company?	
5. What percentage of people understand the influence the business has on the surrounding community and globally?	
6. What percentage of employees "buy in" to the organization's purpose, vision, and values and can articulate what these are?	
AVERAGE SCORE (Total of Rating divided by 6)	

Seven Conditions Assessment Recap

Plot the status of each of the Seven Conditions on the following graph. This should provide a visual representation of where your organization is strong and where some opportunities for improvement exist.

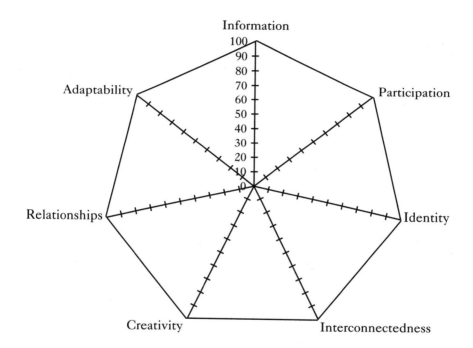

Living systems do not just encompass people—they also include the systems themselves. The systems that comprise the organization are broader in scope than the functional departments or activities and must be understood collectively and independently, and then again as part of an integrated whole. We have identified Six Systems that must be carefully maintained and developed before the organization can thrive.

In a living organization, these Six Systems are the mechanisms that provide the necessary stability and predictability that allow for maximum effectiveness. The Six Systems of Organizational Effectiveness bring about the discipline and numerical controls that add the predictability, consistency, measurement, and accountability required for long-term success within a "living system."

These Six Systems—clearly recognizable in all organizations— include: 1) *Leadership*, 2) *Communication*, 3) *Accountability*, 4) *Delivery*, 5) *Human Performance*, and 6) *Measurement*.

In this chapter, we will not only discuss each of these six systems in detail, but also include guides to help you assess how well each system functions in your organization.

Chapter 7

Mechanisms of the Living Organization: Six Systems of Organizational Effectiveness

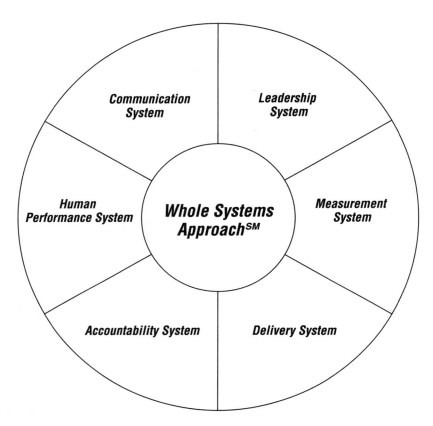

Each of the Six Systems is essential for the organization to run
effectively and contributes to maintaining maximum organizational
productivity. In addition, this simple frame for operating helps organizational members understand how everything is integrated and
identify what is important for success. These Six Systems operate
at both the macro level (organizational) and at the micro level (project or departmental).

Organizations that are continually called upon to conform to new
requirements and expectations require constant "mechanisms" to
ensure they are successful. Organizations facing these constant challenges and restraints must have mechanical measures that allow for
quality control, consistent behaviors, and highly predictable productivity and results. Within these parameters, "control" is instrumental
to a company's viability and profitability.

Systems Are Interrelated

None of these Six Systems is a stand-alone. They depend on each other to function at full efficiency. For example, in order for the Accountability System to be effective, the Communication, Measurement, and Leadership Systems must be fully functional. We can have an excellent Accountability System, but if the Leadership System doesn't model or reinforce accountability, then the Accountability System cannot be sustained. By the same token, it is difficult for the Leadership System to operate effectively if there is no way to measure results or ensure people are accountable for their performance.

The Human Performance System is intended to attract, develop, and maintain talented people. The idea is to hire the best people we can, then help them develop their skills and knowledge over time. Of course, it becomes more and more critical, as they gather additional abilities and know-how, that we retain them as loyal employees. To do this, we must be able to reward them so they feel good about the work they are doing. To reward them properly, we must know what they are accountable for and how they are performing. Thus, for the Human Performance System to meet its objective, the Measurement and Accountability Systems have to function properly.

Another crossover is in how the Communication System affects the Accountability System. Unless people understand what is required of them and unless it is clearly communicated how their actions directly affect the end product (they need this clear line-of-sight), then the Accountability System will be ineffective.

The Six Systems Support the Seven Conditions

The health of your organization, as diagnosed through the vitality of the Seven Conditions, is tightly linked to these Six Systems. Although we consider the Six Systems the more mechanical side of the organization, and the Seven Conditions the organic side, their relationship is synergistic. You can look at the Six Systems like a pacemaker that must function correctly to sustain the health of the living body. For example, until you have carefully constructed a Communication System that works on a mass, as well as an individual, basis, the quality of communications within your organization will most likely fluctuate widely from week to week, and, ultimately, falter in the long run. The same holds true for the other systems and conditions. The mechanical parts must be built with care and tested with regularity before the organism accepts them as its own and thrives.

One of the primary roles of leaders in the new organization is to ensure that these mechanical gears within the organization are machined to specifications and kept well-oiled and running smoothly. Keeping the Six Systems in tip-top shape—and thereby maintaining the vigorous health of the Seven Conditions—should be a daily concern. This involves a constant focus on keeping the purpose, vision, and identity of every individual aligned with those of the organization. Like doctors when they are making their rounds, leaders need to establish a daily or weekly routine of checking to ensure the Six Systems and Seven Conditions are not only coordinated and healthy, but are continually improving.

Each of the Six Systems is described in detail and followed by assessment guides. After reviewing the Six Systems, use the self-assessment guides to determine how well that system is functioning in your own organization.

1. Leadership System: Ensuring Direction and Focus

The Leadership System fosters the conditions under which people can thrive and create outrageous results by:
- Ensuring the health of the Seven Conditions (discussed in the previous chapter).
- Installing the mechanisms for leaders to establish strategic direction, model the desired culture and behaviors, and remove obstacles to help people perform high-quality work on a reliable and timely basis.
- Enabling the creation of meaning within the organization by ensuring everyone understands how what they do affects the goals of the company.

- Allowing people to make sense of the work they are doing and appreciate how and why they are doing what they are doing.
- Helping people understand how the product or service produced by the company positively impacts the community and the world around them.

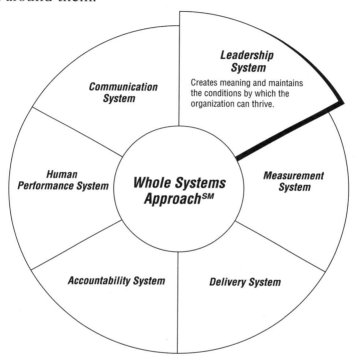

Expectations of the Leadership System

One of the roles of leadership is to engage the organization in a vivid image of a compelling future. To the degree leaders successfully create that image, they can effectively generate change. To the degree they are unsuccessful, change will likely not occur. One way leaders overcome this obstacle is to work to cultivate and nurture the conditions that allow people to utilize their energy, skills, and knowledge to thrive personally and professionally. This means learning to recognize and eliminate obstacles that confront employees or other leaders while providing timely direction. Effective leaders coach, teach, advise, problem-solve, guide, and sometimes issue orders, and they know when to do each!

There is nothing simple about being a leader in today's organization. In fact, in many ways it is far more difficult and requires much more than was the case in "top-down," autocratic companies. In those companies, leaders could bask in the feeling they were in total control. In a living organization, leaders do not have absolute control over much of anything. In some ways, it is like Mr. Toad's Wild Ride. However, for those who have been willing to take the risk, the payoffs, in terms of human relationships, personal gratification, and bottom-line profits, have been the most exciting and rewarding of their lives. *"The Whole Systems Approach* allows you to see past what is, to what is possible," said MichCon's Ewing. "It is a paradigm shift as dramatic as anyone could imagine. Suddenly, the workplace isn't a house of drudgery anymore, but a place alive with hope and excitement."

In a thriving system, everyone is encouraged to develop and exercise their leadership skills informally. It is also essential to designate formal leaders to provide specific leadership within the organization. Executives, managers, and supervisors are traditional examples of formal leaders. These leaders must stay in constant touch with the employees, providing both short-term direction and long-term vision and goals.

We once worked with a company whose employees told us such things as: "Management doesn't have a clue what we do for a living. We're not sure who is really in charge of the organization. Advancement around here depends upon who you know. I haven't a clue where the company is headed. I'm just doing this because I need a paycheck."

These comments are reflective of a Leadership System in need of improvement. This case provides us with a perfect example of what a leadership void creates. Employees are confused, angry, demoralized, and unproductive. Yet, conversations with the leaders would reveal a different perspective—leaders who think they are in total control. Like the line from the movie "Cool Hand Luke," what they were experiencing was a "failure to communicate." When leaders don't communicate—when they fail to lead in the modern sense—sooner or later the company falls into turmoil. On the other hand, a smoothly running Leadership System will yield untold riches, in the form of focused, motivated, and productive employees and a sense of deep personal satisfaction and fulfillment for leaders.

2. Communication System: Enabling the Open Exchange of Information

The purpose of the Communication System within an organization is to facilitate and ensure the transfer of formal and informal information in a manner that is open, clear, meaningful, timely, and believable. The Communication System also:

• Establishes the networks through which information may be openly shared up, down, and across the organization in a timely manner.

• Measures formal communications for timeliness, accuracy, effectiveness, and credibility.

• Shapes and focuses meaning that reinforces organizational strategy.

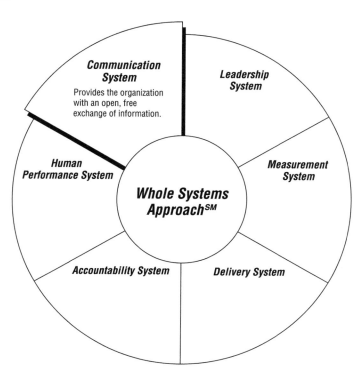

Expectations of the Communication System

An ideal Communication System is one in which informal and formal communications are operating fully within the company. Formal communication consists of structured methods, such as the company publications, networks like video or TV, prepared material sent electronically, e-mails, staff meetings, letters, and memorandums. Informal communication consists of face-to-face, unstructured or structured exchanges of ideas and information. These include any impromptu discussions, whether around the water cooler, manufacturing plant floor, or via the telephone.

Leadership plays a major role in the effectiveness of the Communication System because this system often requires a whole new set of skills. "We had to go to 'school' day and night to stay one lesson plan ahead," said Mark Lerner, COO of GOJO. "When you get to the senior leadership level, old habits can be tough to break. It's easy to make decisions in a command-and-control environment. To move toward consensus-building calls on other communication skills. This especially involves two-way communication. We needed to work on these skills, and still do. It's about strategic communications, and few leaders have those skills already honed. We had to evolve toward systems thinking—thinking with the whole system in mind, rather than maintaining our narrow, functional view. We're using more tools now. We're far more conscious about how we communicate and how our communication affects the whole process."

Among formal communication methods, progressive companies have developed a system through which company-wide communication can occur at any time and reach just about everyone instantaneously. These companies strive to utilize any and all technologies that will make this happen, from the telephone and fax to the Internet and office intranets, TV networks, video conferences, and e-mail. This is primarily one-on-many communication.

But, mass communication is often of less importance than communication at a more local level—one-on-one and one-on-team communication. This communication relies less on technology than on interpersonal skills. Perhaps the most important skill for a leader is the ability to listen. Are we really hearing what the employee or manager has to say? Do we fully understand their problems or concerns? Do we have the coaching and communication skills to teach them how to solve their own problems? A simple formula for the successful transfer of information would include communicating in a manner that is open, clear, meaningful, timely, and believable.

The goals of the Communication System should be kept in sharp focus at all times. It is far more than just a vehicle for leaders to pass along edicts and messages to employees. That, in fact, may be the Communication System's least important role. First, it is a way for employees to build trust and understanding throughout the company. If employees are provided with a constant flow of information they find is truthful and contributes to getting the work done, then trust will begin to build.

At the same time, if the Communication System is open and utilized by everybody in the organization, the identity of that organization will become well-defined in everyone's mind. As people communicate with each other, they quickly gain a "big picture" perspective of what the company is all about. They understand more fully their value to the company because they learn—sometimes for the first time—that others within the company are dependent upon their work. They learn just how their work is connected and why it is vital to what others do. The information helps make the company's identity richer and deeper.

An effective Communication System must provide free and open access to information at all times. Obviously, there will be some proprietary information that must remain secure, but the vast pool of information available to the company should be available at any time to anyone within the company. Open access enables individuals and groups to gather information to carry out tasks and solve their own problems while greatly reducing cycle time. Whenever employees have to request information from leaders, it significantly slows the process.

By allowing employees free and open access to information and the "high tech/high touch" methods for finding it quickly, management is making a strong declaration of trust. "Yes," management is saying loud and clear, "we believe in your skills and your ability to utilize that information appropriately." The reverse is also important; when employees allow leaders full information, they are saying, "We, too, believe in your skills and ability to use information appropriately."

Once trust is established, the Communication System can play a major role in the forming and reforming of the company's internal belief systems. For example, employees may hear they are responsible, but the proof is in an open and effective exchange of information. If the Communication System is functioning properly, employees will not only feel responsible through the Communication System and the free access to information it provides—they will be accountable because any time they see an activity within the organization that runs contrary to the expressed values or beliefs of the company, they have a way to bring this discrepancy to light.

Last but not least, the Communication System creates a competitive advantage. When we have an organization that has grown to welcome information—rather than feel it challenges or threatens them—that organization tends to move forward at an accelerated pace. In the companies we studied, more than 80 percent of the employees and managers often disregarded pertinent data because it threatened them in some way, or they had no formalized system for gathering and disseminating the information. Over time, the results of such disregard can be devastating.

Companies that systematically gather and regard information and make it immediately available to the entire organization gain a tremendous competitive advantage over those that do not. As one CEO observed: "A good Communication System helps us create meaning and purpose out of all the noise." Of all the systems, the Communication System is one of the best enablers to help the organization work smarter, not just harder.

3. Delivery System: Producing Quality Goods or Services

The ideal Delivery System defines and ensures effective and efficient processes through which the organization:

- Meets and exceeds customer expectations.
- Develops process performance standards and quality criteria.
- Establishes mechanisms and guidelines for process improvement, process redesign, and benchmarking.

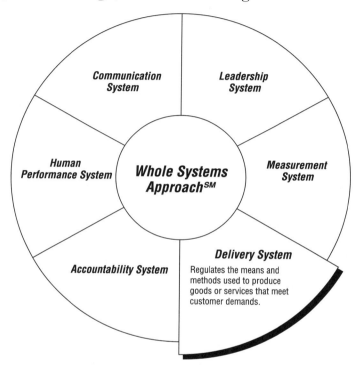

Expectations of the Delivery System

The Delivery System refers to how the company produces and delivers its end product to its customer. On the surface, you might assume this system would be the one system most organizations have perfected. After all, what could be more important than producing goods or services and delivering them to your customers? The fact is, few organizations have a Delivery System that could not be improved significantly.

In the ideal Delivery System, individuals know how their efforts impact product delivery and organizational performance and are able to ensure production success. Employees and managers can create products that satisfy both internal and external requirements.

Downstream requirements are understood throughout the process and upstream fixes are common. A properly functioning Delivery System should optimize an ongoing detection and correction of errors so every area of the organization is functioning effectively at the fullest capacity possible.

Without unnecessary impacts and obstacles, people can make continuous improvement within their area of specialty. Employees feel empowered to take informed action to improve performance. Actionable customer feedback mechanisms exist throughout the process. Together, these contribute to the overall enrichment of the Delivery System; however, individual performance within the organization can only be as good as existing processes allow.

Evaluation and redesign of these processes can lead to increased efficiency and improved workflow throughout the organization. Employee efforts align more directly with company goals, as needed data is effectively collected from available sources, giving more people greater access to appropriate information. An effective Delivery System encourages people throughout the organization to take decisive action that enhances their work and strengthens relationships and results with customers.

Many Delivery Systems don't measure up when the customer demands are factored into the equation. Many organizations do not have a direct line-of-sight to the customer. They don't know exactly what the customer needs or wants. Since the focus and attention are on the bottom-line of the production process, often the customer is lost in the process. The numbers involved with the production of each unit or service often take precedence over the development of the product or service and even over customer demands and needs. Many businesses unintentionally place customer needs second to meeting the numbers. In the long run, the results are almost always less than optimal.

The Delivery System is far more than just ensuring the product or service are provided to the customer on time. An ideal Delivery System embodies the means whereby employees positively affect the creation and delivery of the product or service. It provides the quality practices, tools, and templates needed to ensure the company is yielding service at a standard and price that please the customer. It contains the tools—such as statistical process control, root cause analysis, cause and effect, and action templates—and a procedure for understanding who is responsible for what task and the timeline associated with accomplishing that task.

Obstacles to creating an ideal Delivery System include: outdated technology, poor supplier relations, lack of measures, insufficient documentation, and poor training. All of these things need to be corrected before the Delivery System can work effectively. Few things drain energy, resources, and time faster than having two or more departments unwittingly doing the same thing and, on occasion, even competing for resources such as money because the existing Delivery System does not provide full systems integration and communication. The ideal Delivery System also provides for the integration of the entire system and processes. This eliminates one of the great hurdles of modern companies—the duplication of effort.

4. Human Performance System: Attracting, Retaining, and Developing Talented People

The ideal Human Performance System focuses on the selection, development, training, and retention of the organization's human assets and facilitates the resolution of human relations issues that impede the organization's effectiveness. The purpose of the Human Performance System is to:

• Define and reinforce the specific behaviors that contribute to the productivity of the organization.

• Preserve and enhance the organization's people, resources, and assets.

• Install systems to recognize and reward people as an appreciating asset and a competitive advantage.

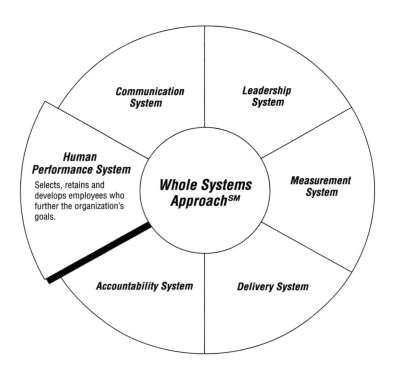

Expectations of the Human Performance System

In a thriving Human Performance System, clear alignment among the following three factors is evident:

• The knowledge, skills and attitudes required to be hired and assume additional responsibility

• The knowledge, skills and attitudes required to accomplish the work

• The knowledge, skills and attitudes used as a market comparison for compensation

People must have a clear understanding of the organization's standard for a job well done and of the value placed on productive behaviors. Employees must trust the organization's commitment to providing basic needs for working productively.

In the ideal Human Performance System, individual and team contributions are seen as the most important product of the organization. Based on this perspective, the Human Performance System must provide the means and methods that motivate people to realize their full potential and become the productive assets they can be in the working environment. People have the potential to be one of the most profitable investments of time and capital an organization can make. In most companies, wages, salaries, benefits, and profit sharing are often one of the most significant budget expenditures. Therefore, the Human Performance System must acknowledge people in the workforce as an integral part of the living organization and provide them with the compensation, recognition, and rewards commensurate with their individual and collective contributions.

A simple equation can be used to illustrate the value of human assets to the organization:

Human Performance Alignment Equation—ICRD=P

Identification +	*Connection* +	*Reinforcement* +	*Development* =	*Performance*
with the purpose, vision, and values of the business	of organizational competencies needed to increase my competencies, skills, tools, and behaviors in my work	in positive feedback that relates to specific results and behaviors	targeted at reaching my maximum potential	leading to outstanding results that can be measured, replicated, and sustained

When the variables in this equation are satisfied, individual performance aligns naturally with the vision and values of the company. People who understand this equation are typically more motivated to excel and contribute significant advances to the organization. Any deviation from this equation can result in people who work outside of the organization's parameters and who may perceive their efforts as just a "job" that is merely a means to an end.

The Human Performance System includes developing organizational competency models that drill down to the individual competency level and are incorporated into compensation systems, reward systems, training, and continuing education programs—all of which are necessary for people to thrive and achieve maximum productivity. The Human Performance System should be designed to reinforce productive behaviors and relationships daily. For example, compensation must be consistent so the company is perceived as fair and trustworthy.

It must be clear to all employees that their productivity has a direct correlation to rewards, and this correlation applies equally in every case.

5. Accountability System: Tracking Individual and Team Performance

The Accountability System clarifies goals and expectations for the organization and individuals including:

• Enabling self-reliance for all organizational members by providing practices, tools, and templates for common language and operations.

• Defining rewards and consequences.

• Administering rewards and consequences.

• Evaluating performance.

• Establishing the environment in which people hold themselves accountable for performance.

• Tracking performance via a system of practices, tools, and templates that apply to each individual and team; managers are no longer needed to fill the old enforcement roles.

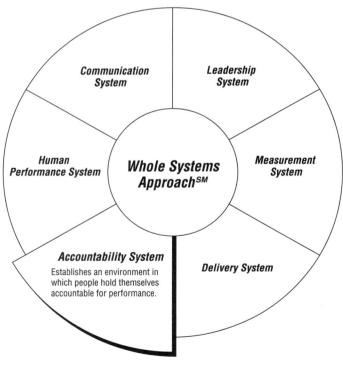

Expectations of the Accountability System

The foundation for the Accountability System is constructed when organizational goals and objectives are communicated effectively, and individuals and work groups understand clearly how their performance helps achieve these goals. Traditionally, company goals were given to a manager, who alone had the "bigger picture." In today's more progressive organizations, everyone needs to understand the larger picture and their place in it. This knowledge makes work more interesting because we can now measure and track our performance so we can be 100 percent accountable to ourselves (and, ultimately, to the organization) for our work product.

An ideal Accountability System links personal performance to organizational goal achievement, providing a line-of-sight from individual and team success to that of the entire enterprise. If employees understand and believe their achievements are tied inextricably to the well-being of the company, they are more likely to "give it their all."

The Accountability System also provides data to the reward system residing within the Human Performance System. Compensation and other rewards—part of a behavior-reinforcing process—should be structured so employee performance that furthers the achievement of organizational goals is rewarded in a meaningful way.

6. Measurement System: Informing the Organization About Itself

The Measurement System allows the organization to inform itself about its performance results by:

• Creating a vehicle through which measurement data may be captured and deployed in a timely and accurate manner throughout the organization.

• Continually refining the sources of data and means of deployment.

• Rolling up measures through levels of the organization so all members can appropriately view and analyze results daily.

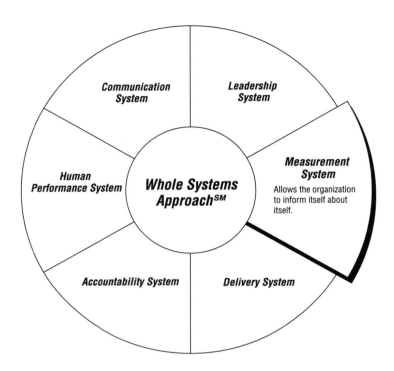

Expectations of the Measurement System

The ideal Measurement System combines detailed findings into groups of summary measures that leaders, teams, and individuals can use to analyze performance (from a balanced perspective). This means that "meaningful measures" that enable the achievement of corporate objectives are provided to the "right people" at the "right time." Meaningful measures are those that initiate action and indicate trends. The right people are those who can act immediately to correct errors at the point of occurrence. The right time is the precise moment when a problem occurs in the process being measured.

The Measurement System is the best tool for organizational self-examination. If the appropriate things are measured (and that is a big "if" in most companies), then the data becomes available for individuals and teams to make fact-based, on-time decisions. The Measurement System is really a decision-making tool. That's what many miss about measurements, believing they simply provide a barometer for how the company is doing. Were revenues up or down? Did the number of units shipped increase or decrease? An ideal Measurement System is far more than that. Using it simply as a barometer is like using a surgeon's scalpel to peel potatoes. It can peel potatoes just fine, but it was designed to do much more.

An ideal Measurement System provides a broad context for us to understand and act on the data it provides. Using it only to measure outcomes is just peeling potatoes. The system should also be used to gather past data as well as capture future predictions. The system should provide a context into which we can place, and more fully understand, all the information it produces—especially real-time data. Thus, we aren't just faced with trying to make sense out of just one data point.

An ideal Measurement System enables us to see and evaluate the process because it is a time-based, whole picture. For example, suppose you are in the soap manufacturing business, and you are having a problem with the production of a chemical for that soap. You need feedback mechanisms to inform you immediately of any problems. If your Measurement System only measures outcomes, you won't realize you have a problem until the customer begins sending the product back. By then, it is too late. This may seem like a simple concept, but many companies have faulty Measurement Systems that create exactly this kind of problem.

Most of the information leaders, managers, and employees need to make critical decisions is derived from the Measurement System. Whenever leaders want to evaluate how their organizations are doing, how any single process is performing, how one area may be affecting another area, whether customer needs are being met, the rate at which products or services are being sold, and whether the company is making a profit, it is the Measurement System that provides the data.

An ideal Measurement System provides focus and instills confidence that our actions are based on complete and accurate data. Without a good Measurement System, we can't focus on results because we don't know what those results are, or perhaps we don't trust the accuracy of the data because it has only been taken from one point in the process.

Remember, what you measure sends a strong message to the people in your organization. What you are saying when you measure something is: This is one of the most important aspects of the organization. For example, if in basketball we decide the only statistic we will keep is rebounds, we send an unmistakably clear message to the players that rebounds *ARE* the measure of success, versus an important aspect of enabling scoring. It won't take long for the important dimensions of points, steals, and assists to be replaced in favor of concentrating on rebounds. It's a natural reaction because if the coach is keeping track of rebounds only, then logically the coach values those players who get rebounds. Deciding what to measure is a more critical issue than most leaders realize. If you do not measure the right things, you inadvertently send a message to your employees about what is important.

Leaders and companies often have Measurement Systems in place that measure the wrong thing! For example, companies will do things like measure the number of calls per hour received by their service representatives rather than track the number and impact of problem resolutions or solutions recorded per hour by these same representatives. In this instance, the emphasis is on how many calls are fielded, not the quality of the interaction.

Many years ago, we worked with a major Midwest hotel chain's reservation center that had 300 people answering calls. The company's Measurement System consisted of supervisors randomly standing near each phone with a stopwatch. Reservation agents were measured on how fast they dealt with the customer and hung up. There was no measure of how often agents sold rooms. Instead, the Measurement System provided a scenario where the customer became the obstacle to the reservation agents' performance. The faster the agents could dispose of those pesky customers, the better!

We invited the company to shift that emphasis. Instead of measuring the time the agents spent on the phone with their customers, the organization began to measure whether the agents made the sale of the room or resolved other customer-service related issues. The results were immediate. The attitudes of the reservation agents made a 180-degree shift toward their customers—now their goal was to please customers rather than bump them off the phone. Within five weeks, sales rose dramatically. Management attributed the increased sales directly to the modifications of what they were measuring.

Six Systems Integrators: Common Language

We continually encounter discord around the definition of terms that have been interpreted in vastly different ways. This lack of common definitions—of a common language—leads to confusion, conflict, and ultimately, inefficiencies, and a loss of productivity. The same thing can be said for the lack of common practices, tools, and templates because they form the "common language" for people in the organization to understand each other.

When Moby Dick first burst above the ocean spray, Captain Ahab was astonished. "That's one big fish!" he must have been thinking. But Ahab had nothing on most organizational leaders when they first comprehend the enormity of their company's communication issues. We once worked with a task force of leaders in a multinational, direct-sales company that was attempting a major change effort to "empower" its employees. Top management thought the effort would be accomplished in record time because its intentions were overwhelmingly positive. After all, what employee would object to being "empowered"? But the effort stalled. When asked to intervene, our first action was to meet with a large group of managers—all of whom readily used the term "empowerment" to describe their efforts. We asked them one simple question: "What exactly do you mean when you use the term 'empowerment'?"

The three hours of heated discussion that followed made it abundantly clear why the organization's change effort had stalled. There was no common agreement on what "empowerment" meant. This was astounding to the senior leaders, who had assumed everyone defined the term in the same way. In reality, the definitions ranged from one end of the continuum to the other. Some thought empowerment meant employees—in the form of work teams—could control their own budget, jobs, and projects. Others thought empowerment meant employees could control their time, including when they came to work and when they left. Still others interpreted empowerment to mean employees could choose between a number of benefit options and plans. Yet another faction believed empowerment simply allowed employees to freely voice their opinions on how work was accomplished but that management still made all the decisions.

Awash in this tidal wave of differing and debilitating opinions about what "empowerment"meant, the CEO sat shaking his head. He was stunned by the whale of a problem that had been hidden below the surface of the organization for so long. Like Ahab, he may have been saying to himself: "That's one big fish!" Creating a shared definition simply requires conversation. In its absence, confusion prevails.

Another example of the need for shared understanding and common language occurred recently in a hospital system where senior leaders had committed to a project they called a "turnaround." We gathered senior leaders in a room and asked them to tell us how they defined the term "turnaround." The variety of answers shocked everyone. Some thought "turnaround" meant the organization was in a crisis mode, requiring desperate, radical measures to survive. Others felt "turnaround" meant a bit of budget tightening was in order, like cutting back on napkins and crackers. Still another group felt "turnaround" meant laying off hundreds of people. It was clear that without a shared definition of what "turnaround" meant, the turnaround had the potential to become a very expensive guessing game and fodder for the rumor mills. Unified change was impossible.

Common Practices, Tools, and Templates

One of the key integrators in the Six Systems is the sharing of common, organization-wide practices, tools, and templates. This allows people within different divisions and departments—many of whom may have never met each other face-to-face—to work effectively together. Great inefficiencies within the organization are often the result of various functional groups using varying and, sometimes, conflicting work methods. When there is a common set of practices, tools, and templates that everyone uses, inefficiencies in the organization can be substantially reduced.

A good example of the confusion that occurs in a company often has to do with not having a shared understanding or a common practice around holding a meeting. At one of our client sites, each department had a different way of scheduling and conducting meetings. As long as they didn't cross departmental lines, protocol was clear. The confusion arose when people from two or more departments were to meet. The simple clarity provided by the development of a single tool that would unify their meeting process and provide a common template allowed the organization a shared framework in which to operate. This simple tool and template helped focus and align the organization and shortened the time required to accomplish multi-department tasks. Today, most employees can walk into a meeting anywhere in the organization and understand the process and the language used. Not only does this allow for goals to be accomplished at an accelerated pace, it greatly increases the rate at which change occurs.

A "practice" specifies the guidelines for choosing task teams or managing a project. The "tool" used to help manage the particular project might be software such as Microsoft Project™, while the "templates" might include a team meeting agenda form. Whatever the specific practices, tools, and templates used, the key is to embed them throughout the company to bring the organization together on common ground. Many times, these common practices, tools, and templates become a new proof point for the "way we do things" in our new culture.

Working at the Project Level

The Six Systems are inherent at the project level as well as the organizational level. As much of the immediate work is done at the project level, the functionality of the Six Systems is as critical there as it is at the higher, organizational level. Let's say, for example, we create a team to improve the cycle time for delivery of a product to our customer. When the project team comes together, they need to know who will assume the leadership, what results they want, how those results will be measured, what the timetable will be, how each person will be held accountable, how the product will be delivered to the customer, who will perform which tasks, and what competencies, education, and training are necessary to do the job.

For example, before a task team launches a project, the team must consider the impact of the project on the other Six Systems and ensure those systems are represented in the process of defining, developing, and launching the project. This includes determining how the team members will communicate with each other and with people who might act as advisors to the project. It is critical to realize the Six Systems are a working framework that needs to be applied at every level—especially the workgroup level or wherever the work actually is accomplished. Ensuring the Six Systems are in place and fully functioning will help project teams reach their goals with maximum speed and efficiency.

The Ultimate Goal—Thriving People

If the Six Systems are in place and the health of the Seven Conditions is solid, you will realize a work environment where people can grow personally and professionally, experience quantum leaps in productivity, and are less likely to take their skills and expensive training to another company. Often during the change process, people experience personal transformation and discover renewed energy, excitement, and, yes, even passion for their work. It's a dynamic and sometimes volatile mix that creates a challenge for leaders to channel and harness that energy, excitement, and passion.

Six Systems Informal Assessments

To assess the current state of your company's Six Systems, respond to the following questions on a scale of 0 to 100 percent with 100 representing a fully functioning system. Anything less than 70 percent should be a call to action and indicates a need for improvement.

Leadership System Self-Assessment

Question	Rating
1. What percentage of the leaders in your company provide a compelling overall focus and direction for the organization?	
2. What percentage of your leaders exemplify the company's vision and values in ways that serve as an inspiration to everyone committed to those ideals?	
3. What percentage of time do leaders in your company make available all information that might be useful to employees in getting work done?	
4. What percentage of the company's leaders actively seek to understand the reality of the workplace, rather than gravitate toward information that is "packaged" correctly or that comes from favored sources?	
5. What percentage of leaders focus on improving organizational processes and mechanisms rather than placing blame?	
6. What was your overall Seven Conditions recap score (page 95) as this is a Leadership System rating?	
AVERAGE SCORE (Total of Rating divided by 6)	

Communication System Self-Assessment

Question	Rating
1. Do executives, managers, and supervisors communicate a consistent story of the purpose, vision, values, and strategy of the company?	
2. When information comes to an employee through formal channels, what percentage of the time has the employee already heard something about the issue "through the grapevine"?	
3. What percentage of the time are formal communications believed?	
4. What percentage of your employees feel their voices are heard and their concerns respected?	
5. What percentage feel they are encouraged to continually exchange information?	
6. What percentage of employees would say they are "fully informed" about company happenings?	
AVERAGE SCORE (Total of Rating divided by 6)	

Delivery System Self-Assessment

Question	Rating
1. What percentage of the people within the company clearly understand how their actions and work affect the work of the other employees?	
2. What percentage of employees clearly understand customer requirements and expectations for the goods/services they produce?	
3. What percentage of the employees could articulate their work processes?	
4. What percentage of work processes are regularly measured for effectiveness?	
5. How would you rate your company in terms of technology, especially in areas most critical to building competitive advantage?	
6. What percentage of employees have been given the knowledge and tools to improve their work processes?	
7. What percentage of employees understand how the company makes money?	
AVERAGE SCORE (Total of Rating divided by 7)	

Human Performance System Self-Assessment

Question	Rating
1. How would you assess your company in terms of the skill and productivity of your employees?	
2. How does your company rate in terms of the alignment between the criteria used for recruitment and hiring and the company's vision and values?	
3. What percentage of people have a clear and consistent sense of the organization's expectations for their work?	
4. How does your company rate in terms of whether the employees trust the organizational commitment to providing ongoing development?	
5. How would you assess your company in terms of the competencies required to meet future demands such as market competition?	
6. What percentage of employees are clearly aligned with personal and organizational goals as they accomplish their work?	
AVERAGE SCORE (Total of Rating divided by 6)	

Accountability System Self-Assessment

Question	Rating
1. What percentage of the time do employees try to avoid accountability versus accepting it and producing real results?	
2. What percentage of the time do employees play a key role in evaluating their own performance?	
3. What percentage of employees play a key role in evaluating the performance of leaders, including those in the highest positions?	
4. What percentage of employees are able to quickly access the information they need to make sure their decisions are consistent with the organization's priorities?	
5. If asked to identify the three top priorities in their work, what percentage of employees would respond quickly and definitively with statements directly related to the organization's overall goals?	
6. What percentage of employees have the tools and templates to "manage" their team, their work, and their results?	
AVERAGE SCORE (Total of Rating divided by 6)	

Measurement System Self-Assessment

Question	Rating
1. How well does your organization's culture support the idea that all employees should generate and use measurement data regularly?	
2. What percentage of your organization's measures are regularly evaluated and updated?	
3. How well does your organization measure results linked to organizational performance, individual/team/unit performance, and process effectiveness?	
4. How closely are the measures your company uses aligned with the company's vision, values, and critical success factors?	
5. What percentage of managers and leaders see measurement as a tool to enable better performance rather than as a means for punishing those who don't produce?	
6. What percentage of people in your organization can discuss what any specific measure/indicator means in the context of overall business results and direction?	
AVERAGE SCORE (Total of Rating divided by 6)	

Six Systems Assessment Recap

Plot the status of the Six Systems on the following graph. This should provide a visual representation of where your organization is strong and where it could improve.

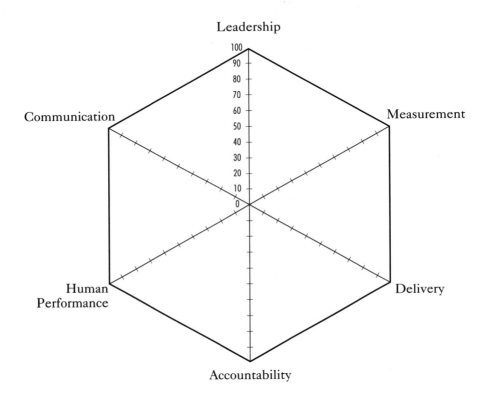

Experience has proven it is possible to develop higher levels of trust through aligning individuals and the organization to a common line-of-sight. Crucial to this premise is ensuring each person in the organization has a legitimate voice in critical areas of the company, including how work is accomplished and decisions are made.

The Alignment Model serves as the cornerstone for the transformation process, extending from the individual and the team to the entire enterprise. Many organizations begin their transformation

Ensuring a Line-of-Sight to the Customer: The Alignment Model

initiatives by focusing on restructuring, rearranging the boxes on the organization chart first, later discovering that they still face the same issues because culture always supersedes structure.

The Alignment Model can be used to educate the organization, teams, and individuals about which areas to explore and align with next, depending on work that has already been accomplished. For example, if strategy has not been expressed, process has nothing with which to align because strategy informs process. Likewise, process then informs structure and so on. Mixing up the order is tantamount to "placing the cart before the horse."

Alignment Model

**Business Imperative/Reason for Change
(Stakeholder Input, Feedback, etc.)**

Purpose, Vision and Values

Critical Success Factors &
Business Declarations

Strategy

Process

Structure

Team &
Individual
Performance

Stakeholder Results

The top of the funnel is as wide as possible to allow maximum input and a wide scan of all information. As the organization works down the funnel, alignment becomes more focused, moving from the global to the specific and from the organizational perspective to the individual task level, team alignment, and individual coaching. When the organization arrives at the bottom of the funnel, participation is clearly visible through individual contribution. By the time the organization is "aligned," every person involved has the opportunity to establish a true line-of-sight to the customer and feel directly connected to and in sync with the organization's goals and vision. In this chapter, we will specifically discuss the building blocks essential to alignment. In the next chapter, we will discuss how to use the Alignment Model to ensure each person has the opportunity to have an authentic voice in the process.

This model is a macro/micro model, meaning you can use this model as an individual and with a team, a department, or an entire organization. For instance, if my vision for myself is to be a marine biologist, then I will have very specific strategies for appropriate schools and will likely need to structure my life in an area where the ocean and sea life are easily accessible. I won't be doing this at the community college in Dallas, Texas, or living in Palm Desert, California. To align to a vision, everything must work to support that vision, and you are the person who works it.

Many people have never taken on a full-blown whole systems change effort but have used this model successfully in aligning their team or their unit. Sometimes change comes a step at a time, and it is important to focus on where you have influence and can make a difference, rather than reject the whole process because "it's too big" or "my company would never do this." As you review this Alignment Model, keep your specific sphere of influence in mind rather than focusing solely on the entire organization.

1. Articulating Organization Identity: Purpose, Vision, and Values

At the very top of the Alignment Model are those things that constitute organization identity—purpose, vision, values, history, culture as it exists today, and, in many cases, the reason people are loyal to and choose to stay with the organization. Purpose is the reason for being and answers the question "Why do we exist?" Vision represents a compelling declaration of a future we want to create and are committed to create collectively. Values are the principles we embrace as an organization to guide our actions; the non-negotiable code of conduct for the team or organization.

An example of a purpose, vision, and values statement is the one our own organization articulated.

Maxcomm Inc.,
Purpose • Vision • Values

Purpose
• Creating a world of work where people thrive!

Vision
• Honoring *Whole Systems* and *Inherent Potential*^{SM} as the context through which all thinking and action take place.

Values
• We trust each other, our processes and the system in which we are working.
• We honor the flow of the systems we enter—we find out what is working and establish common ground.
• We align our intentions and actions.
• We believe diversity springs from a shared base of competencies and the art of practice.
• We play full out.
• We form partnerships that produce lasting value.
• We hold that the health and well-being of the system is paramount.
• We regard information as a source of growth and learning.
• We leave whatever we touch better off than we found it.
• We refuse to create or operate within a false economy.
• We multiply and leverage all our efforts.

Many popular business books, including *Built to Last* by Collins and Porras, provide details on how to formulate these statements and document the value of creating a shared purpose, vision, and values statement.

2. Defining Organization Performance Criteria: Critical Success Factors and Business Declarations

Critical Success Factors are the defined elements necessary for achieving purpose, vision, and values and, thereby, serve as targets around which the organization can formulate measurable goals. They provide the means for translating the vision, values, and purpose into business plans and integrating them into the daily work lives of the people within the organization. There is no " right" or " wrong" set of definitions here. Each company develops its own. The Critical Success Factors are industry-driven and vary from organization to organization, unlike the Seven Conditions and the Six Systems, which are universal across all organizations. Generally, Critical Success Factors are also used as the overall categories for the Measurement System. Some companies have added things such as communication, recognition, results, and quality service. Some include more behavioral targets such as decisiveness, leadership commitment, role clarity, and talent.

The Critical Success Factors are key indicators that must be monitored continually. They can be compared to the gauges on your automobile dashboard control panel—they reflect what is occurring internally in different areas of the organization as the change effort moves forward. Although your organization will define its own Critical Success Factors, general factors include financial and operational, employee well-being/stakeholder satis-faction, information access and disbursement, market leadership/customer satisfaction, and quality effectiveness.

All organizational members should agree upon these Critical Success Factors so everyone is "pushing in the same direction." Defining these Critical Success Factors is invaluable in helping people articulate and agree to the key elements that will drive the organization's success in the future. These are the elements to be measured to provide a comprehensive, high-level reading of per-formance. These Critical Success Factors serve as pillars around which your organization can formulate the Business Declarations.

Business Declarations are commitments to outcomes the organi-zation currently does not have the means to accomplish. They con-tain the "stakes in the ground" that propel a company to heights it would not achieve without the stated intention.

Critical Success Factors and Business Declarations are not clubs to hit ourselves with but rather motivators to elicit the best from us. As strategic work continues and more people become actively involved with the change effort, these factors assume a greater meaning and become cornerstones for developing strategy.

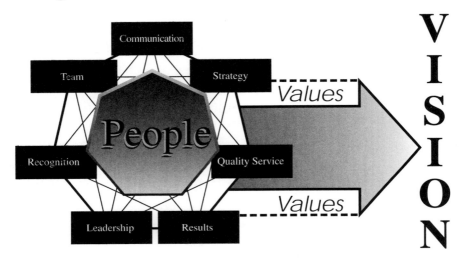

MichCon's Critical Success Factors

3. Defining Organization Direction: Strategy

This is the strategic thinking for how to realize the purpose, vision, values, critical success factors, and business declarations of the enterprise. Strategy involves understanding organizational core competencies and then developing strategic goals (where are we going?), the approach (how are we going to get there?) and tactics (what actions are we going to take?). Together, they form the strategic plan of action for the organization.

Core competence is the capability—a bundle of skills, technology, and intellect—that underlies leadership in a range of products or services. Most valuable are those competencies that represent a gateway to a wide variety of potential product or service markets. A company must be viewed not only as a portfolio of products or services but also as a portfolio of competencies. Some of the very best

---

Sony
- Core Competence—Miniaturization
- Custom Benefit—"Pocketability"

Federal Express
- Core Competence—Logistics Management
- Customer Benefit—"On-time Delivery"

Wal-Mart
- Core Competence—Logistics Management
- Customer Benefit—"Choice, Availability, and Value"

EDS
- Core Competence—Systems Integration
- Customer Benefit—"Seamless Information Flow"

Motorola
- Core Competence—Wireless Communication
- Customer Benefit—"Untethered Communication"

---

explanations of Core Competencies are provided by Hamel and Prahalad in their book, *Competing for the Future.*

Examples of Core Competencies and Customer Benefits include:

Core competencies are the organization's strengths. These need to be nurtured and protected at all costs. Core competencies strongly influence strategic goals and should be articulated before addressing strategic goals.

The strategic goals depend upon the identified core competencies—the ones we have and the ones we need—and, to some degree, on the industry and direction your specific company must take. In today's environment, these strategic goals should be out three to five years in term and structured to be measurable, concise, and time-bound. These strategic goals should provide strategic direction that includes understanding the marketplace, accurately forecasting changes in the marketplace and industry, and positioning the organization for the future.

Once the Strategic Goals are established, the approach for accomplishing them must be developed. In other words, how can we get there? Approaches are the core methods to achieve the goal. One approach may be discarded for another if the approach is not working or a more effective method is discovered. On the other hand, the goal is enduring and selected because of its vital nature to the overall strategic direction.

Developing the tactics and articulating critical issues for implementing the strategy is the final step. Tactics are the actions required to implement an approach and can be accomplished, modified, or changed quickly. They are short-term events along the path to achieving the goal. Critical issues are the "show stoppers" that must be addressed within a short period of time for the enterprise to succeed. For example, in one organization, the technology department was in such disarray that it required immediate attention before the realignment could move forward. The success of the realignment was dependent on technological support.

4. Creating the Transportation Vehicle: Process

Throughout the organization, people have the ability to impact the production and quality of company products and services either positively or negatively by the way they think, work, and interact with other people in the organization and with customers. Individuals need to know how their efforts influence the accomplishment of internal and external work requirements to ensure they manage their own performance to guarantee successful results.

Process involves how the work gets done end-to-end—all the inputs, outputs, and key activities. Completing this work is based on a shared understanding of common terminology.

Once basic core processes are identified, they need to be put together in an Enterprise Map. This map serves as a tool that provides a visual representation of how work proceeds through a series of major, high-level functions and flows across the organization. The completed Enterprise Map of basic core processes should link to the goals, scope and objectives that support the company purpose, vision, values and other essential business strategies.

The entire process can often be best defined through large-group participation. This is where momentum truly begins to build to a critical mass when shifting to and realizing a new culture.

5. Building the Foundation and Supporting Architecture: Structure

Structure is the organizational framework in which the company operates. This is how work is organized and informed by processes, strategy, business declarations, critical success factors, purpose, vision, and values. The key understanding about structural alignment and its positioning in this approach is that structure does not determine process, but the other way around. Under traditional change efforts, where small management teams design the entire change without consulting the employees, this is a difficult, if not impossible, concept to communicate to the employees, who are shut out of the process. In this way, there is increased "buy-in" because employees are not only part of the change process but also responsible for making the changes a success. In other words, we live with what we create. We are responsible to ensure it works!

Common sense tells us that an organization should be structured around how work is actually done; however, common sense is often lost in tradition. Tradition says "structure" is the "organization chart." The chart, which clearly showed the hierarchical ladder, defined the organization. The higher up the ladder you were, the more important you were. Spans of control were what internal organizations were all about then. Few employees, save a senior leader or two, had a clear line-of-sight to the customer. Employees' lines-of-sight started with themselves and ended with their closest supervisors.

Beautiful but Useless Boxes

Despite the drawbacks of a rigid organizational structure based on the traditional organizational chart, most businesses still depend upon them for definition and security. Organization charts do provide a quick definition for reporting relationships, but when used in a way that is set-in-stone and power-based, they can be likened to razors that have lost their edge—they still "look" good; they just don't work very well anymore. Of all the outdated elements of the mechanistic approach, the set-in-stone organizational chart, representing power instead of how work gets done, has been one of the most difficult to shed. Psychologically and emotionally, many leaders have a tough time letting go of the security that those clearly defined boxes provide.

Recently, we asked a CEO of a small New England corporation to draw an organizational chart of his company. He spent five to ten dedicated minutes sketching a complex chart, with his name firmly in the top box. Then an incredible thing happened. We asked the employees in the room what was missing from the chart. The response was unanimous. "Us!" they cried. The CEO, while painstakingly mapping a complicated pyramid of five levels of leadership within the organization, had forgotten to include the employees.

"How often," we asked the employees, "do any of you pull out this organizational chart to get work done?" Everybody laughed. Not one hand was raised. The CEO had spent ten minutes drawing beautiful, but useless, boxes. For some employees, it was even worse than useless because they felt it humiliating to see their names left off.

"Who do we look to please in this chart?" we asked. "The boss!" they shouted. "Who does the boss look to please?" we queried. "His or her boss!" they responded. "Who is looking to please the customer?" we continued. Silence. Yes, we look to the boss, not necessarily to the customer who is obviously missing from the page. With a focus on the customer and line-of-sight, the Alignment Model is played out in the structure that is created.

6. Realizing the Purpose, Vision, and Values: Team and Individual Performance

Individual and Team Performance addresses the collective and individual competencies, accountabilities, rewards, and recognition required to thrive. Competencies are identified during the process and structure work. The work at hand now is making it work—where the "rubber meets the road" with each individual in the organization. At this point in the alignment process, the organization will need to implement new roles and modify them as needed to ensure maximum productivity. Just as the Measurement System should be structured to indicate how the organization is performing, an individual performance scorecard should be developed to reflect how each individual is performing so compensation can be integrated to support all the work.

Additionally, by this point in the alignment process, each process, unit, and team is typically applying the Alignment Model to their own team and individual tasks. This ensures a direct line-of-sight to "what we do" and the impact we have on the enterprise and its results. We also have a direct line-of-sight to our customers, as a group and as an enterprise, because we've now done the work to ensure linkage all the way through the system. One organizational member put it this way: "Every time we follow the Alignment Model in our team, we save time and get results. Every time we think we don't need to follow it or can skip some steps, we end up coming back to it." When this realization is apparent, individual and team results begin to soar.

Where to From Here?

The goal of the Alignment Model is just what you see at the bottom of the funnel—a smile on the faces of stakeholders and customers. This funnel should provide a binocular view for everyone in the company so they can see customers and stakeholders—close-up without obstructions. Alignment adds tremendous clarity to every member's work and connects him or her to the overall process. Each company will use this model in a slightly different way, to meet its own needs, but the model is designed precisely to provide such flexibility.

This model will continue to be useful throughout the change process and running the business phase as an integrator for team planning and chartering and organization review. The Alignment Model will best come to life through an employee involvement process, which ensures alignment is sustainable.

Changing and
Running the Business:
Whole System Phases
of Transformation

The final component of *The Whole Systems Approach* represents a "how to" sequential perspective and groups actions in the process by time-bound phases. The phases apply regardless of where the organization is in a change effort. In some cases, the phases can be used like a road map to bring together a transformation effort already in progress. In other instances, the phases can be used to launch a new initiative. Regardless of the status of the effort, it is important to honor and capitalize on the good work every organization already has in process and avoid duplication of effort.

This chapter introduces the complete change effort process from beginning to end. If the process seems overwhelming at times, remember that applying even a few aspects of the process has greatly benefited a number of companies or work units. For example, many organizations have chosen to conduct an annual results or customer conference without using the entire conferencing process to align their organizations. They simply want to use this technique as a way to reestablish a customer focus and gain common ground for the coming year. As you read this chapter, we invite you to open the scan of possibilities and then sort through what could or would work for you, your group, or your organization. In other words, just because you see and smell the whole enchilada does not mean you have to eat the whole thing, particularly in one gulp!

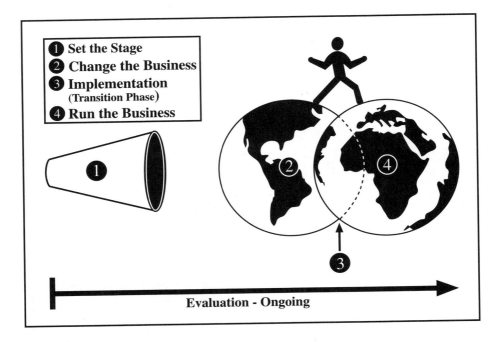

One of the first actions an organization needs to take is to identify the specific goals it wants to accomplish and then work back
through each of these four phases. Because each organization is
unique in its culture and outlook, many outcomes of this process
will be different each time it is followed. What is universal and
moves this process forward is the attention to and inclusion of the
previous three components.

We have found that focusing on the Six Systems is particularly
key during the first two phases. In addition, all of what is currently
occurring within the organization must be integrated. This allows
the organization to capitalize on work that has been accomplished
while encouraging those people who are already vested in the
future state to buy in quickly. Most importantly, the Six Systems
provide the mechanisms to allow connection to the whole so people understand how their activities contribute to the organization's
objectives and outcomes.

To receive maximum benefit from using this approach, ensure
you or another "designated" person (internal or external) has the

jurisdiction that will be required to see this effort through and the full commitment of leadership to stay with the effort. If you don't have the expertise needed to safely navigate through the required changes, find it. Using facilitators from both inside and outside the organization is very beneficial. This does not imply the approach is externally driven, but an external perspective that is both objective and experienced is advantageous in most cases. This external help can range from limited to extensive, depending upon the needs. Minimally, external help is valuable in grounding and aligning leadership. The ratio of externals to internals depends on the capacity, capability, and credibility of internal resources. Whenever possible, internal resources should be used, with the external support bolstering them where necessary.

Set the Stage: Capturing the Organization's Attention and Focus

The purpose of the Set the Stage phase is to prepare the organization for the upcoming changes. It is important to recognize that the people within the system are responsible for sustaining anything new and eliminating anything that needs to be changed. Nothing will happen for long without their engagement, commitment, and support. Now is the time for leaders and influential people within the system to prepare themselves to hear the voice of the organization and capitalize on it rather than disregard it. Stage setting is exactly what the name implies—ensuring the backdrops are ready and the basic education with "amplified" communication about the effort is in place. Once the stage is set, it is key to capture the organization's attention and focus before the process of building self-reliance can be accomplished through organization involvement.

Time and experience are the determinants for using "new theories and practices." If, over time, individuals in the organization are encouraged to use something new, continue to have a good experience with it, and are reinforced for using it, it will be retained as part of "how we do things around here" until it becomes habitual. However, if leaders do not keep the focus on the new, the system will almost always revert back to how things were done in the past.

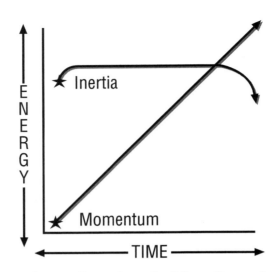

Change the Business: Creating the New Organization

The Change the Business phase involves launching the actual changes. The first apparent change begins with treating "the organization as leaders." This means engaging employees in conversations and decisions that would generally be reserved for "formal leaders." The change period is filled with revamping and installing the Six Systems and Seven Conditions and ensuring alignment through the use of the Alignment Model. This means a substantial shift from "how we are today" and typically results in finding creative ways to "increase capacity" to ensure systems are in place and can be maintained over time. Identifying and understanding your organization's capacity is key to navigating through this phase.

Resource Mix—A Key to Building Self-Reliance and Organization Capacity

Most organizations share two things in common—they are doing "more with less," and they are working "over capacity." No longer is there as much discretionary energy or time available in any organization as there was ten years ago. By conservative estimates, organizations are working at 110 percent to 125 percent of system capacity. When the system is over capacity, too many things are left undone, and the organization's members do not receive the satisfaction of finishing anything. New starts are seen as a burden and destined for problems prior to initiation. Even worse, new starts become a way of life without achieving completion of anything. Existing problems are over-dramatized, and people become caught up in everyone else's business instead of tending to their own responsibilities and finishing their daily tasks. Generally, though, if an organization is working "over capacity," it is not necessarily "over capacity doing the RIGHT things."

Money, people, and time are the three major resources available to any organization. Over the last two to three years, a significant shift has occurred. As a rule, money is no longer perceived as the major resource constraint. Time and people have become the greater challenges to resource management. How often have organizations spent the money to purchase something new without allocating the time or people to capitalize on the purchase? How often has an organization spent the money to develop a plan, yet invested very little in focusing on how to implement it?

Add a change effort to these capacity issues and the combination has the potential to be deadly, if not properly managed. Any major change involving the whole organization will add another 20 to 30 percent. This 20 to 30 percent increase is critical to understanding what it means to "live in the present" while at the same time "building for the future." As organizations are already operating in a deficit, being "real" and acting in a capacity-building manner are key factors for the ultimate success of any change effort and ensuring self-reliance over the long term. Communication is also critical, as is focusing energy on completion by factoring in system capacity.

For example, an internal Information Systems (IS) group in a manufacturing organization was failing their mission and corporate goals. They had recorded most of the required standard operating procedures and developed the protocols and project management skills to accomplish their mission. In addition, they had a significant amount of "new" software that had yet to be installed. All of these tools were of value and desperately needed; however, they sat in the storage facilities of the building "unopened." Unfortunately, this IS group did not "have the time" to use what was available to them.

Understanding existing capacity and building a culture that takes pride in completion is part of the answer. In addition, it is critical to be proactive enough to increase and expand capacity. This requires time and forethought. To maintain a reputation as a quality service provider, organizations must invest in excess capacity in advance of any attempt to increase sales volumes or find ways to limit customer growth to remain within its existing capacity. This situation is common in the organizational world of today.

In one instance, an information outsourcing firm made a conscious decision not to accept any new customers until they could ensure there were no bugs in the system and their current clients were completely satisfied with the level of service they were receiving. As a result, the sales pipeline was virtually shut down for over a year. This could have spelled disaster for the organization; however, the leaders were so confident they could build capacity once they had stabilized the business, they resisted the temptation to accept any new contracts. Once the focus on customer service proved to be on track, it required another year to start the sales pipeline flowing again. In the space of five years, this organization grew from an entrepreneurial startup to $160 million in sales. This growth would not have been possible had the leaders allowed sales volumes to increase without establishing the foundation and developing the resource capacity beforehand.

Engaging the Organization in Designing the Future

Once resource capacity has been addressed, it is time to begin "changing" the business. During this phase, one of our primary tools for employee involvement is the introduction of the conferencing process. Conferencing is a methodology that allows people to learn from firsthand experience what is going to happen and why. Concerns and questions can be addressed immediately rather than being permitted to fester and build into silent resistance. This process also generates excitement that can sweep people along in the movement, engaging their hearts and their minds while concepts are still fresh and exciting.

The conferencing process provides the vehicle to engage large numbers of people in the system and bring them together in one room at the same time to discuss topics germane to the organization. Those topics include the areas identified in the Alignment Model—the direction of the company, how work should be accomplished, and what structure will best support that work. As part of the conferencing process, it is vital that customers, suppliers, and all stakeholders are represented and are a part of the discussions. Customers, in particular, play a critical role. Leaders are often reluctant to allow customers to help change the organization. Nothing threatens their perceived control as much as giving customers an uncensored look into the organizational processes. "They'll see us, warts and all," complained one CEO with whom we worked closely. "We won't be able to control what information gets out to them."

He made this observation despite the fact the organization had nearly 300 customer service representatives talking to customers every day of the working week, all year long! Once we pointed this out to him, he realized his vision of control was a myth. In reality, there is no perfect script. Customers gain information about organizations in a myriad of uncontrollable ways. It is a waste of time worrying about what they might see inside the organization, warts and all. The truth is, they already have.

The willingness to be open and deal directly with customers is what has fueled the amazing growth of Dell Computers, according to CEO Michael Dell.

Leaders who have mustered the courage to face their customers have invariably been glad they did. "It was a completely energizing event for us, even though they told us some things that were tough to hear," said Mark Lerner, COO of GOJO Industries, Inc. "Some messages have become rallying cries within the company. For instance, one customer stood up in a Vision Conference and said: 'You haven't thrilled or delighted me in the past five years.' That became a 'Remember the Alamo!' kind of statement for us. It was all the more powerful because it didn't come from management, but from the customer.

"Another customer noted that our competition comes primarily from Fortune 500 companies. 'What happens when that 1,000-pound gorilla wakes up and wants to eat your lunch?' the customer asked. Well, the '1,000-pound gorilla' catch-phrase stuck within the company, giving us a wonderful wake-up call. It's amazing what happens when you listen to your customers," said Lerner.

The value of having every employee appreciate what the customer needs and perceives "firsthand" when they interact with the organization cannot be overstated. As one leader observed, "I have been saying this stuff for years, but when I speak, it only goes to the front row. On the other hand, the customer's comments penetrate all the way through."

In every whole systems conference we've facilitated, higher quality relationships emerged when employees, customers, suppliers, and stakeholders participated without scripting. Order emerges naturally in these conferences, without control. Attempts at controlling this interplay can stifle the energy and productivity that spring from the conferencing process. The order comes from a focus on agreement, common ground, and what works. To some, the loss of control can be a physically painful experience. However, if they have the commitment to see the process through, the pain quickly disappears and is replaced by the remarkable results that follow. We should note the conferencing process can be modified to engage employees without using "large group methodology." This can be accomplished through a series of modified "mini-conferences" using the same conferencing principles applied on a smaller scale.

Using Conferencing to Move Through the Alignment Model

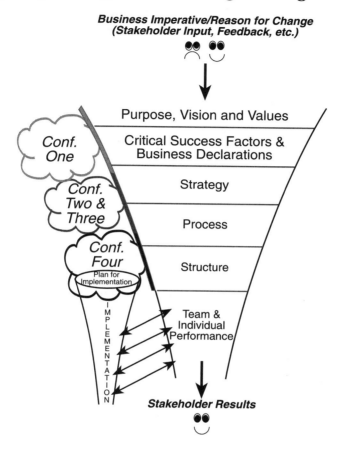

During the Change the Business phase, we generally conduct a series of four large group conferences. Each conference includes participants who represent a comprehensive cross-section of people within the organization and a mix of external stakeholders—people who reflect as much diversity as possible. When brought together in situations that create opportunities for mingling and interacting, large group conferencing provides a critical mass of agreement and support to fuel the intended changes.

When coupled with the Alignment Model, conferencing rapidly changes an organization, team, or work unit while achieving outstanding results in the process. To ensure success, participation of individuals in actual conferencing events should always be voluntary, and the typical conference environment must be devoid of organizational politics. Depending on the size of the company or work unit, the ideal is to directly involve at least 30 percent of the people as participants over the four conferences. This can mean conference sizes ranging anywhere from 100 people to more than 600 participants in each conference. Literally every voice in the organization needs to be tapped.

The first conference, a Vision Conference, introduces the work of changing the business in a powerful, open forum. Stakeholders are encouraged to participate in discussions and respond to ideas with personal questions or observations, rather than feeling as if a pre-established plan is being imposed upon them. In this first conference, participants work to create a compelling future they will commit to seeing through in action and are actively engaged in developing and accepting new ideas for change. This gathering is not a time to dump one-way information; it is a time for all the participants to share, discuss, and contribute to the upcoming changes.

The conferencing process fosters discussion, raises numerous questions about the organization, and provides a forum whereby employees begin to grasp how they will engage with the proposed changes and how the approach works. They begin (some enthusiastically, some reluctantly, some cautiously) to realize they have a voice—as well as a responsibility—in how this turns out. The definitions that ultimately make up this organizational identity lay the foundation for the rest of the process. This is accomplished, as the Alignment Model suggests, by ensuring a wide scan that includes marketplace and customer input and feedback and by articulating the business reason or imperative for change. We work with these components, like a painter on a canvas, until

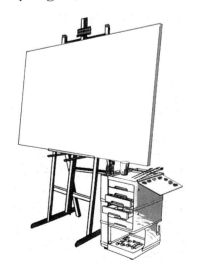

we have a clear picture of how everyone collectively would like the organization to be. This picture of the new organization becomes the unified vision among employees, managers, vendors, and customers. This unification process isn't always unanimous at first, but through the conferencing process it becomes a "united rally" for common goals and shared understanding.

The second and third conferences, Process Design Conferences, involve identifying how the company currently does business and considering ways to meet strategic goals and improve the company's position in the marketplace. Usually by this time, the change process is well underway. People are more comfortable with the conferencing process, even though they may still feel some discomfort with their own participatory roles. Members are given process tools and education to then develop "as is" and "should be" process models. This involves plotting how we do work now versus how work should flow to be optimally effective.

By the end of the Process Design Conferences, participants understand the motivation and analysis behind the "should be" process models because they were actively involved in developing them. They should have had ample opportunities to comment on and, ultimately, ratify these models. This makes member "buy-in" of the models much faster and easier because they have been part of the design process. They know and feel part of the work and the company. They know what they think and do really does make a qualitative difference for themselves and the growth of the company.

They also gain a much deeper insight into what makes the organization run, and where and why it needs to change to succeed in the future. This "eagle-eye" viewpoint—and feeling of ownership for the changes—are not only tremendous motivators, they also arm employees and managers with the enhanced perspectives, insights, understandings, tools, and process steps that allow them to make better choices when it comes to improving their own work processes.

The fourth conference in the series, the Structure Conference, ends the Change the Business phase by creating an agreed-upon structure and a comprehensive implementation plan for putting all of the change design and commitments into action. A move to implementation marks the beginning of the Transition the Business in the transformation effort.

Structure is typically a "hot button" in organizations. Usually much work must be done to prepare leaders and the organization for a different view of structure. For example, one client observed, "When we made the determination to become a customer-focused, team-based, process-oriented and results-driven organization, it changed the entire landscape for us. We literally burned the organizational chart because it was holding us back. We were a growing organization, and we wanted to continue to grow. We didn't want the weight of the organization—the practices, procedures, rituals, and rigid structures—to inhibit us from growing in terms of size and profitability.

"But, we didn't get there right away," this same client cautioned. "Our intent wasn't to do this as a restructuring exercise. We followed the Alignment Model where we defined our purpose, vision, values, critical success factors, and strategies for achieving these things. We did a tremendous amount of work in this process, and it wasn't until after this that we got to structure. By the time we got there, we found that each of the elements required to become a customer-focused, team-based, process-oriented, results-driven organization represented a serious shift from a structural standpoint. Although initially there wasn't a conscious effort to change the organization's structure, it doesn't look anything like it did when we started out."

A similar transformation took place at First Security Information Technology, Inc. (FSITI). "We went from a traditional, hierarchical organization chart to a very flat, non-traditional, and almost undefinable structural design," said Karen Wardle, who worked as a project manager at FSITI. "It was an enormous move for us. This was a conservative banking institution, and we were all nerds to boot, but when our customers told us that we were nearly irrelevant, we realized with some shock that we were not getting the job done under the conventional structure."

Through the process, an entirely new organization emerged. "We still had the CEO and a leadership team underneath him, but they were the business, vision, and values people now," Wardle said. "People were grouped by skill sets to accomplish many business projects, and leadership of those projects would vary based on the team's decision. Our terminology for our varying supervisors was 'sponsor.' Depending on what project you were working on, you might have a different sponsor each time. Also, no sponsor had 100 percent say over our performance, salary, or work design. We developed an evaluation process where peers, team members, business partners, customers, and sponsors all had equal input. It was a radical, invigorating, and liberating change."

Some companies are attempting to restructure solely around process, but many, like GOJO, are also centered around functionality and customer focus. "Customer focus was huge for us," said Mark Lerner, COO of GOJO. "For example, we restructured our sales and marketing division and consolidated our sales force to present one face to our customers. That required a massive structural change. To better serve our customers, we also went to a supply chain concept that caused a radical change to the organizational chart. Now, the supply chain cuts across historical functional boundaries; ultimately we ended up as self-directed work teams."

The key element here is deciding how work flows and defining the roles necessary for each employee to play in order for tasks to be performed. When you answer the question of how work is done, structure will emerge naturally. Defining how work gets done determines how employees interact, thus defining their roles and their relationship to each other and the work. "People really do have a say at FSITI, in an honest and open environment," said Wardle. "The changes in our work roles were the results of formulations around process, and because we had a direct say in how that was done, we took full ownership of those changes."

The integrity of that structure requires that those people who actually do the work be included in its design and implementation. Some time ago, a senior leader in charge of 2,000 employees inside a health care insurance company brought in a major consulting firm to design a new organizational chart and structure for the company.

The consulting firm was paid a lot of money to work with 15 senior managers over a six-month period. During that time, they literally redesigned the entire company. Proud of their accomplishment, they revealed the chart to senior leadership. Everyone was excited until they tried for nearly 18 months to sell the changes to the employees. Then they realized they had a huge problem. After two years, the employees still weren't buying the new structure. Implementation was at gridlock.

"We made a mistake," the company's COO told us. "The senior managers were so excited to be drawing up the plan that we never even considered employee involvement. Now we're paying the price. We've never overcome it. We've spent two years trying to convince people this change is good for them. It's a hard, hard sell."

The story underscores a major difference between traditional change methods, which must be "sold" to employees, and an employee involvement strategy that sells itself. By involving employees, they perceive the changes as something "We did to ourselves because we believe in a new future" instead of "They did it to us" or "They stuck it to us."

The conferencing process does not end with determining structure and developing an implementation plan, however. Once the implementation plan is in place, all employees begin the effort of making the plan work. Much of this is done through additional mini-conferences focused on specific areas or needs of the organization.

Transition the Business: Implementation

Implementation is the transition from changing to running the business. At this point in the change process, systems are partially in place, and the momentum for change is building. People are "open" to new ways of doing things but have yet to become accustomed to "doing" them in the new way. The organization has a plan, but the plan is only on paper. Although people may be anxious and unsure of the how, they understand the direction in which the company is moving. When the Change the Business phase winds down and the Transition the Business phase gears up, systems must move from the experimental arena into "real time."

Transition is like trying to run on a sidewalk while pouring the cement. You now have your feet in both worlds and must make a decision to jump before you "split" trying to hang on to both. The organization needs to integrate all of the pieces that have been put in place. Different from the windstorms of transformation during the Change the Business phase, the objectives for the Transition the Business phase are to ensure all systems are established and that common tactics, tools, templates, and practices are ingrained into the culture to provide infrastructure and continuity while allowing the business to grow.

This period of transition is defined by focusing attention on integration, implementation, and completion to evaluate which systems are in place and being utilized effectively throughout the organization. Integration, implementation, and completion are all key words that define this phase of the transformation. Integration, implementation, and completion are the focus; common beliefs, practices, and tools are the means.

Integration

Integration is about "connecting" all the learning and thinking of the organization and applying it through the discipline of practice. Integration is necessary to ensure all the conditions of change have been synthesized into the working environment. These conditions prepare the organization for accepting the new blood that will give it new energy and life. Learning happens fast; integration occurs more slowly. Many organizations suffer from a predisposition to be thoroughly analytical to the point that the organization suffers paralysis and inaction; therefore, integration, stops . . . unless a crisis develops.

The Transition the Business phase is about preventing a "crisis mentality" for "overdesign." Unfortunately, the tendency to design, design some more, analyze the design, discard portions of the design, redesign, and redesign the redesign are all too common. The way to break that cycle is through implementation. "Organizations learn only through individuals who learn. Individual learning does not guarantee organizational learning, but without it, no organizational learning occurs," noted Peter Senge in *The Fifth Discipline Fieldbook*. Learning is the key to a company's success because only when individuals integrate ideas can they apply those principles within the organization and move toward established goals.

Implementation

Implementation is about "breaking the design cycle" and determining "good-enough" planning to begin testing. In other words, implementation is about "experiencing" the plans of the Change the Business phase by living them through and working out the bugs. Traditionally, organizations have not always encouraged learning that enlightened or enriched the whole company. Individuals have been sequestered in emotional compartments and physical cubicles from which they collected or processed information parceled out to them in a piecemeal fashion. Learning in organizations means the continuous testing of experience, and the transformation of that experience into knowledge—accessible to the whole organization, and relevant to its core purpose. Knowledge comes through practice and experience—actual implementation.

Up until this time, the organization has been like a student in a sailing course, learning the basic maneuvers and practicing with ideas and plans with minimal "gut wrenching." During the Transition the Business phase, the organization needs to pull out of the old world entirely and apply what it has learned to the realities and currents of the new world so it can pull up the anchor and sail on the open water. Much of this work is accomplished through employee involvement in smaller unit and process conferences and intact work teams. This is important because sharing ideas and discussing various possibilities opens up "potentialities" that can make the difference in important elements of implementation that have lasting ramifications. This is also critical because it ensures integration at the very time some people become too entrenched and lose opportunities or miss what others are doing.

Interactive relationships between members, once discouraged in business settings as a waste of time, are now considered valuable contributions to the company's progress. It's what Brook Manville, Director of Knowledge Management for McKinsey, terms "internal knowledge on demand." That is, creating the ready ability to tap into what people have learned—and creating the motivation to put such learning in touch with other people and information. Ensuring forums for "connection" and "evaluation" of the effort is critical.

Completion

Completion is about "finishing and celebrating." Endings are as important as beginnings; yet, they often go unrecognized or unacknowledged inside our organizations. Completion is used to honor the organization's work and ensure the "ritual of endings" at the end of the Change the Business phase. This also includes ensuring lessons learned are carried forward.

When all of the systems are implemented within the organization, completion of the "change" has occurred and Run the Business has begun—at this point, informal leaders at all levels are exercising control over their own facilities. Formal leadership is unified and mastering important skills for leaders in this "new" organization, and all employees are utilizing new skills.

At this point, an organization must have internalized the language of concepts and ideals essential to change. This language gives voice to the company's short-term and long-term goals, based on their purpose, vision and values. Without that internal dialogue constantly reinforcing and connecting every member of the organization, precious concepts are not articulated, processes result in inefficiencies, and the motivation of members can be lost.

By its own actions, a company determines whether these systems are truly integrated into the working consciousness or if they are merely artificial tools that can be discarded when the familiarity of old behaviors lures people away from what they have learned. If the organization can expand upon what it has developed to this point, it can take steps toward achieving its goals. As the company moves from one step to the next, the foundation of common practices, tactics, tools and templates can be used to lengthen its stride in the right direction. Successful steps can be repeated, even though the organization may stumble and fall on occasion. With practice, the muscles of every member are strengthened; each person can identify and maintain his or her balance. This self-reliance provides the whole organization with the energy and drive to move steadily toward achieving established goals.

The Transition the Business phase is complete when all systems are integrated and essential tactics, tools, and practices have become second nature. When various milestones have been achieved; efforts and successes have been acknowledged and celebrated; and the organization's pride in, continued recognition of, and focus on accomplishment is apparent, the company is ready to enter the next phase—Run the Business.

Run the Business: Making it Habitual and Sustaining the Change

Once the Transition the Business phase is complete, the focus must be on sustaining the new behaviors and building the core competence of self-reliance. This comes through application, experience, and reinforcement. If all of the tools, templates, and practices are in active use, people will learn to apply them in more situations and grow more confident and competent in their use. Leaders have to continue to constantly and consistently model and reinforce through their actions and deeds.

The shift is from being novices at the "new" to being high performers. This is easier to do if the change has been consistent with how we want to run the business. Often the belief persists that if we can just "get through this situation," things will go "back to normal" so we can "get back to work." It must be clear going in that this approach fundamentally changes the perception of how business is done. Doing business this way will become the norm and there will be no going back to the "good old days."

Every self-reliant organization includes coaches, mentors, and teachers—people who help others build skills and capabilities by developing new practices and tools that help make the theories practical. In the Run the Business phase, there are generally many "simple" things that need to be practiced; however, this is the tough part. Sometimes as individuals, we do better with things that come and go than we do with incorporating lifelong disciplines. Consider dieting, exercise, and meditation as a few examples. The discipline and rigor required to make these practices lifelong habits are the very same discipline and rigor required to run the business after a change has been installed.

Sustaining the Results

A critical difference between *The Whole Systems Approach* and others currently available in the marketplace is that whole systems technology can be used to run the business long after the changes are in place, thereby creating sustainable results and more organizational self-reliance. In many cases, once a change effort runs its course, it is cast aside as an aberration. *The Whole Systems Approach* represents a process that can become part of the DNA in the organization. This approach fully balances business results with process.

In creating enduring results during the Run the Business phase, it is critical to maintain attention and focus on ensuring the running of the business is consistent with the changing of the business. For example, if large group participation technology is used to change the business, then participation should be used to run the business as well. Participation and conferencing are means to achieving the desired outcomes, not ends in themselves. They are tools only, not end goals. Participation—particularly large group conferencing—is not a panacea. Merely gathering folks in the room without thoroughly addressing "the stuff" that integrates the work will not get the job done. The same focus on resources used to change the business must be maintained in running the business. Once something is running, people tend to think it can run on its own. This is rarely the case.

Involving customers in the process is critical. Every enlightened leader and manager will enthusiastically attest to the importance of involving customers. It's a difficult thing at first—this face-to-face powwow with the people who buy your product or service. But, it soon becomes clear to those going through the process that customers are essential to this approach. Going in, most leaders are apprehensive about involving stakeholders; yet, every single time stakeholders have been included in the process, the organization has come away with a "win-win" for everyone. Undoubtedly, all organization members will experience an emotional roller coaster as changes occur. As these changes are not typically cosmetic or procedural and often range from a major change in work roles to potentially life-altering changes in the way we view ourselves and our relationships with those around us, this approach will challenge all cultural assumptions and many very personal ones as well.

This approach is not episodic in nature. It is not event-driven, but rather outcome-driven with the focus on the overall context for any event that may occur and organizational integration with other activities and initiatives. This approach is not based on the use of one method or tool. Clearly, this approach utilizes a variety of theories, tools, and technologies for accomplishing its mission. This approach provides an overall framework for integration and results and can be used as an umbrella for several other approaches. It serves as an integrator for capitalizing on "what works" and can be utilized alone or integrated with other initiatives.

This approach does not eliminate the need for management and leadership. In fact, when organizational members assume more accountability and responsibility, leadership needs to step up and assume stronger, if different, roles than in the past. As much as we might want to believe effective organizational change can occur without the involvement and commitment of senior leaders, it won't happen. Commitment from senior leaders is vital. The approach will not work without it; however, smaller efforts can have successful results as long as the senior leader will allow the designated "departmental leaders" the space they need to manage their areas! Many leaders, consultants, and internal agents often miscalculate the amount of energy and focus any major change effort requires. Changing an organization consumes tremendous energy and demands persistence. Leaders who have been involved in this approach will tell you: "It was the best thing we've ever done, but I can't ever remember being this tired." The personal fortitude and commitment to see a major change effort through can be as personally challenging as they are exhilarating.

Evaluation: Assessing Organizational Self-Reliance

Periodically throughout the process, formal evaluation of the organization is required to facilitate course corrections and decisions regarding dedicated resources to continue the work and ensure organizational self-reliance is being created. When the resources of time and people are committed, then change can be sustained through new habits. In this way, the organization is more self-reliant and can feel satisfied with what has been accomplished. For instance, a client recently created a position for the leader of organizational communication to ensure communication changes were sustained. Confidence is high that communication will continue to be maintained and enhanced in this organization, given the commitment that has been made to it being self-reliant.

Another organization had the opposite experience with sustaining its communication system. A large utility client invested significant resources in a formal "communication system," only to let the investment die a slow death by not replacing resources when key people left the organization. Over a period of less than one year, employee satisfaction levels dropped dramatically, and believability of communication went from a high of 92 percent to a low of 51 percent. After reinstating the communication system and providing sufficient resources to staff it appropriately, the believability index has risen to only 63 percent; the lost time has cost the organization dearly.

In the end, remember the wisdom the sage Yoda offered to the young Jedi warrior Luke Skywalker in "The Empire Strikes Back." After learning the methods and techniques of the Jedi, Luke told his teacher and mentor Yoda he would try to put them into practice. "Try?" retorted Yoda sternly, "There is no try. There is only do and not do!"

Section
III

**Realizing
Inherent Potential
through Personal
Alignment**

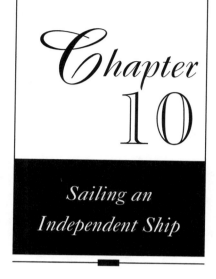

Now that you have an understanding of the components of *The Whole Systems Approach* and what occurs during this process, it is time to "get personal" by addressing the current morale inside organizations and how a new legacy is not only desirable but necessary. For many people, there has never been a more opportune time to embrace a new vision of leadership and work.

Chapter 10

Sailing an Independent Ship

The 1990s became the decade of corporate disillusionment. Many of us, as Baby Boomers, grew up watching our parents spend their lives with one or two companies and then retire gracefully due to a company's generous retirement plan. Corporations, in that respect, were once looked upon as "trustworthy." They upheld the unwritten social contract that called for employee loyalty in exchange for a secure work environment. During the past decade, unfortunately, one single word has not only broken that trust, it has obliterated it beyond recognition. The word that strikes fear in the hearts of most employees is "downsizing."

The Broken Contract

Downsizing has come to characterize much of what is wrong with the mechanistic, top-down approach to business, not to mention the greed of the past two decades. People are clearly seen as pawns to be sacrificed in this great chess game that captivates investors, owners, and "the players" on Wall Street. Downsizing has become the euphemism for the arbitrary firing of sometimes tens of thousands of employees. It represents a complete and total betrayal of the unwritten social contract. Downsizing, perhaps more than any other phenomenon, lays bare the ugliest side of the "depreciating," mechanistic approach to business. Employees are seen as nothing more than removable, replaceable components. If profit margins aren't pleasing investors or if stock prices dip, current, popular change efforts have one simple solution—lay off 100, 1,000, or 10,000 workers. Whatever makes the numbers right!

In the short run, this remarkably mercenary approach creates results. Wall Street usually reacts favorably while investors are told by corporate leaders: "We're taking steps in a positive direction." However, the long-term results are often disastrous. We are only now beginning to appreciate just how devastating this approach can be. Along with job security becoming a thing of the past on a global scale, employee loyalty, trust, inspiration, and passion have fallen victim to the fallout from downsizing. Downsizing, and the paradigm it represents, makes it impossible for all but a few people to find a sense of safety and passion in their work. It destroys hope and injects a deep-seated resentment among employees that sometimes can never be eradicated.

This shift in loyalty is critical because no organization can reach its potential unless its people are inspired about their jobs and their futures. The inspiration comes from a personal alignment with a compelling organizational purpose and vision coupled with confidence in the leadership of that organization. The passion comes from having a voice in how the organization is run—knowing you are valued, making a worthy contribution, and believing your ideas have been heard.

The ironic part of this popular downsizing trend is that often the problems that caused the company to falter are rarely addressed or solved through this strategy. Usually, downsizing is a desperate move made to cover up years of bad decisions and poor habits by the leaders of the organizations; yet, it is rarely these leaders who lose their jobs. Instead, they make a "financial decision" to create a "leaner-meaner" organization by firing people who were, in many instances, not part of the problem in the first place. In most cases, the top leaders remain, and the employees, both those who stay and those who leave, have a clear view of the dark and capricious side of leadership. It's often an image they don't soon forget.

The New Contract

A more effective way to increase a company's bottom line is through employee involvement. Massive downsizing is usually not the answer. If downsizing continues at its current pace, we will suffer the ripple effects from this dreadful experiment for years. The result of poor management based on a century-old paradigm where the employees pay the price is what happens when the ship never leaves the harbor.

The Whole Systems Approach not only repairs this broken contract but also serves as the basis for drafting a completely new one. One of our primary goals has been to establish an environment in which individuals and the organization can "thrive" and manifest potential through results and personal fulfillment. This means we have to find a way to reestablish a new level of trust between the organization and its people. This also means we have to find ways to enhance individual and organizational self-esteem.

When employees have experienced "a significant emotional event," such as downsizing, whether they stay or go their levels of self-esteem and trust flounder. If they are "downsizing survivors," they typically feel bad they are staying when so many other "worthy" people were sacrificed. In the process, somehow those who are left become the "betrayers" and part of the "betrayed" at the same time. If a person is let go, he or she ends up suffering from feelings of incompetence, anger, and "Why me?"—all of which can contribute to lowering one's self-image.

According to Nathaniel Brandon, author of *Six Pillars of Self-Esteem*, self-esteem is comprised of confidence in facing life's challenges and a sense of feeling worthy of happiness and fulfillment. In a downsizing situation, "survivors" rarely feel "worthy of happiness and fulfillment," while those who are downsized rarely feel confident to be successful in a new organization that may, in fact, do the very same thing to them again!

Building trust and self-esteem is critical to unleashing inherent potential. The personal development of every employee is instrumental in the organization's success. Individuals need to understand their roles within the company and how important each is. They need to know how and why their contribution is crucial to the organization.

The new social contract between the organization and the employees calls for an entirely new understanding of responsibility and roles. Employees must be viewed and treated as the heart, soul, and brain of the organization. They must be given a legitimate voice in how the organization runs and be expected to use that voice. In order to accomplish this, extensive work is needed to align organizational and personal goals. This is essential because the creation of similar goals and vision creates fertile ground for trust to grow and flourish. If we are all striving for a common goal or objective, we can only achieve the end if we work together and are clear on our goals, roles, and procedures. As a result of this process, we will be far more likely to trust each other.

Trust also grows when people feel respected and valued. That is a primary outcome of giving people a legitimate voice in how their work is done and is indicative of a respect for the value of thoughts and ideas. Likewise, when we feel valued, we are more willing to trust ourselves and our instincts. We feel competent in our ability to achieve results and make wise decisions and feel worthy of fulfillment and happiness at work. We then increase self-confidence—our own and the organization's—and find ourselves taking pride in self and our work community.

As this occurs, a subtle shift happens in how managers and employees begin to view themselves in their new roles. Under the old, top-down paradigm, most were not given a voice, nor were they given much responsibility. If you give someone a job description, that's usually the only work they will perform. In that regard, employees have received "entitlements" in the past, although those entitlements have come at a significant price. In effect, employees have been treated like children, who are asked to do specific chores around the house while not being "burdened" with the family's bigger financial picture. While that may be appropriate for children, it establishes an unhealthy and ultimately unproductive relationship between adult employees and leadership.

Healthy adult relationships are based on individuals placing issues on the table and dealing honestly with whatever they are required to work through. Healthy organizations operate in much the same manner. That is why *The Whole Systems Approach* places the burden of the organization's financial health squarely on the shoulders of all organizational members. Frankly, employees have as much at stake in the future of the company as leaders do. In exchange for the added liberty of having a legitimate voice in how the organization is run, employees typically assume individual responsibility for the company's bottom line. The mind-set changes from one of entitlement to one of ownership. This is a crucial shift that changes everything, from the way people think about their work and their relationships with others in the company, to the way they think about themselves.

The new contract calls for new beliefs from leaders and employees and for employees to take on a new level of responsibility for themselves and their work. Everyone in the organization must become self-reliant, seek new solutions to problems, and assume the company's well-being as their personal responsibility. Ultimately, every employee must be encouraged by peers, leaders, and organizational systems and procedures that reward creativity and innovation. Employees must willingly face the fear of sharks so they can sail their own ships out of the harbor.

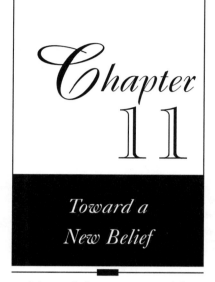

Chapter 11

Toward a New Belief

Over the years, most of the leaders we have encountered were convinced their companies needed to change; yet, the changes they implemented, or had implemented, were clearly not going to accomplish the desired outcome. At first, we were confused about why such intelligent people would invest so much time and effort on change efforts that were clearly not positioned for success. After interviewing several of these leaders, we realized they were not successful because they were trying to change the company without changing their own beliefs!

It is critical that as *The Whole Systems Approach* is introduced "organizationally," everyone understands that "personal" transformation will be required. Leaders, too, must change many of their old belief systems that are getting in the way of what they really want. We adhere to the time-honored truism: *You will achieve only that which you believe.* If leadership's thinking is constrained to the dogma that work is drudgery, that personal fulfillment at work is just a pipe dream, and that employees can't think strategically and must necessarily park their personal selves at the door, then that is the result they will realize. Their thinking has to change from the belief that work is about spans of control, daily stock prices, and hierarchical power structures. In order for effective change to occur, leadership has to believe in something far more invigorating and compelling. To be an effective leader and to implement real and enduring change, leaders must believe, at their very core, that a world of work where people and organizations thrive is possible.

The Myth of Absolute Certainty

A principal reason so many struggling organizations are resistant to this type of change springs from a powerful and deep-seated desire on the part of leaders and managers for control and pre-dictability—no surprises. The roots of this vastly limiting desire run deep. The earliest and greatest threat to prehistoric man were the wild, unpredictable elements of nature, whether in the form of floods, wild animals, hurricanes, earthquakes, or other natural cata-strophes. These were daily threats to people for thousands of years. No doubt much, if not most, of the collective energy of humankind has been expended in an effort to control nature and its seemingly chaotic tendencies.

During the past century, of course, nature has become far less of a threat (in fact, the threat has been reversed), but a new form of super-conservatism has taken its place. Investors, clamoring for secu-rity, have passed on their fear of uncertainty to organizational leaders, who have responded by embracing a short-term focus to running their organizations based more and more on "calculations." This mathematical, emotionally removed model is highly intoxicating because it gives the illusion of certainty, control, and predictability. When a company is viewed from a strictly linear perspective, it is easy to be seduced into believing you can control and predict the out-comes simply by adding and subtracting variables, such as people or inventory. With this lens as the only lens, the equations are simple. More employees means more product; fewer employees means less overhead. What goes into the system determines what comes out of it: a world of total control of mathematical equations.

In recent times scientists, with the help of supercomputers, have debunked this "theory of certainty." They have found that even mathematical representations themselves do not produce straight lines on graphs. Most experienced organizational leaders are the first to admit there is no such thing as certainty in an orga-nization. Anyone who has ever worked on the floor of a factory, or within a company, will tell you the same thing—that isn't the way things really work. Still, the desire to control, to predict outcomes, remains a powerful narcotic.

Shifting Views on Control, Order, and Chaos

By now, you have a good idea that *The Whole Systems Approach* shifts the way most of us view control, order, and chaos. The old view, held almost universally at one time, was that organizations could not work efficiently without a firm chain of command and definitive spans of control. The entire company and all its daily processes had to be under strict control from the top. Losing that control meant chaos, and organizational chaos was about the most frightening proposition most leaders could imagine.

But, this effort at total control comes at a significant price. First, it makes the organization clumsy. Decisions have to go up and then back down chains of command that sometimes include anywhere from 10 to 15 people. The entire process is painfully slow. At the same time, control leads to low-esteem, an uninspired work environment, and, in many cases, turned-off employees. Factions develop easily and office politics rage out of control as people continually maneuver for turf, power, and covert "revenge."

There is usually little or no alignment of vision, purpose, and values between employees and the company. Each employee harbors a separate vision, usually centered around how he or she can gain a greater span of control or perhaps escape the wrath of an over-bearing manager. Is it any wonder people count the number of days to retirement?

The fear of chaos is so great, leaders and employees alike are willing to sacrifice organizational speed, adaptability, and energy; the inspiration and greater productivity of organization members; and the results and unifying force provided by a common vision and direction.

The great irony is that such control is mostly an illusion anyway. Many of us still foster, to some degree or another, this fear of chaos and believe absolute control is possible and desirable. A case in point is a project involving a major consulting firm determinedly trying to develop accounting software they believe will control every possible strategic and financial scenario an organization might face. They've been working on it for three years, and predictions are it won't be completed for another two.

Such software doesn't stand a chance. There simply is no way you can control every variable in a living organization. The movie "Jurassic Park" illustrates that point in graphic fashion. The park developers, driven by their confidence in superior technology, believe they can control the random elements of nature. The random and chaotic laws of nature prevail, as the dinosaurs reproduce outside the park, even though they were "reengineered" to be sterile. The short-sighted park developers met a fate not too dissimilar to what often happens to control-minded corporate leaders. They were chewed up and swallowed by the very forces they sought to control.

Order, Not Control

Although we can't control a living organization any more than we can control nature, we can establish processes within the organization that allow it to adapt and thrive, regardless of the variables thrown its way. What we are seeking in the new organization is order, not control. All natural systems live and grow on the edge of chaos. Chaos is a constant part of our lives every moment of the day. In fact, life would be rather boring without it. Once we understand and accept this fact, chaos begins to lose the shroud of mystery that so alarms some of us. Not only should we not be afraid of chaos, we should be eager to take advantage of the powerful, natural energy attached to chaos. If harnessed correctly, that energy can add incredible momentum to an organization and its people.

When the 1989 Loma Prieta Earthquake roared through the San Francisco Bay Area, leaving chaos in its wake, thousands of people self-organized into small groups—without official orders or control—to help each other. Even the second wave of relief—ambulance drivers, fire fighters, and other official rescuer workers—didn't wait for the mayor to tell them what to do. They followed basic strategic guidelines developed earlier, but they also reacted intuitively and almost instantaneously to the individual and random disasters wherever they occurred.

They reacted in a natural way, making split-second decision that enabled them to save lives and property. Think, for a moment, how a mechanistic organization would have dealt with this crisis. Rescue workers would have stood around for hours while a strategic planning committee labored to put an action plan into place. The plan would then have been studied for many more hours by several layers of officials. Meanwhile, the fires would have raged out of control and lives would have been lost.

Organizational chaos can be the very best energy source available to your company. Some who have experienced this energy would bottle it if they could as a "precious substance." For example, one employee told us his favorite time in the change process was when it was the most "chaotic" because that was when the organization was also the most creative, energized, and fun. "There were no limits," he said, "just ways to get it done!"

We know that for many people this journey from the old "home base" to the "new territory" causes a lot of anxiety. The best way to describe it is through the following model:

The Home Base Model

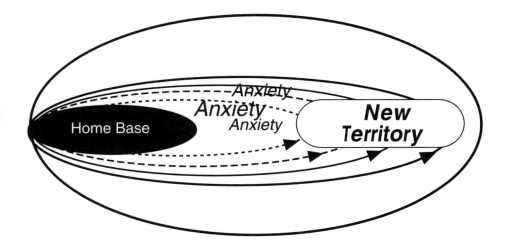

ase" is where we feel comfortable—existing in the
/erything is familiar. We feel safe and secure. When
ιy from our home base, our body gives us some auto-
nou.   ːk in the form of a small jolt of adrenaline to our systems. This ιɔ our body's way of telling us to stay alert, just in case
some saber-toothed tigers are out there waiting to pounce on us.
But, when we repeat an activity three times, the body recognizes
the activity as no longer new. Our internal feedback systems do not
pour adrenaline into the body any longer, and we no longer experience a heightened sense of alertness. The activity is now part of our
known territory. We've been there or done that before. Thus, we
have expanded the size of our home base. The once new and
strange is now familiar and known. The more one ventures out of
his or her comfort zone, the bigger the new comfort zone becomes.
This is the personal growth process everyone encounters in trying
on new beliefs and acting "as if" until they really do become "who
they aspire to be."

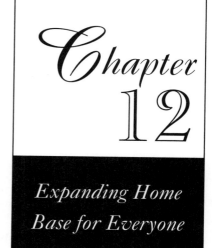

Chapter 12

Expanding Home Base for Everyone

The Whole Systems Approach is based on a total involvement strategy of planned change. All organizational members are considered participants in the change process, meaning all members can help shape the future design and direction by having direct input into decisions—such as how customers are served and by whom, how results are measured, and what strategy, policy, tactics, structure, and operations are best for accomplishing their own work.

When we ask employees, "How many of you want a voice in the way the organization is run?" we get an eager show of hands. "Yes," most say, "we want that opportunity, that chance to have greater influence." They are sometimes surprised but always delighted to be given more voice. But at the same time, they feel a far greater sense of responsibility and accountability than ever before. At some point, employees clearly understand that this opportunity comes with a price tag. With voice comes responsibility and ownership of results. In some companies, fewer than half of the employees will, at first, embrace their newly found liberty and responsibility. This is okay. The momentum and energy created by those who do embrace this responsibility are more than enough to sustain the organization and encourage others along the way.

"When we first underwent the change effort, I estimate that only about 20 percent of the employees and managers were ready for this environment," said MichCon CEO Ewing. "Then there was a small but discernible group whose idea of success was to hold on to old ideas. They wouldn't budge, even though our move from a regulated to a de-regulated company had changed everything. The largest group fell somewhere in the middle. They moved toward where the strongest voices were, where the most compelling arguments for stepping to the right or to the left were advanced. That was our job—the leaders' job—to make those arguments repeatedly, clearly, and tangibly. We had to be convincing that the way to move toward the future was not to try to hold on to the past."

Shifting the culture means expanding home base for everyone in the organization and redefining the roles of leaders, managers, and employees.

Authentic Leadership

Leaders become "walking examples" of the organizational vision, purpose, and values—and they must still make critical decisions. Authentic leadership is gained through respect, not through position. It is based on an authority given freely by followers, not by the CEO or owner of the company. As organizations flatten and become more team-based, the need for authentic leadership does not decrease, as some might think. Instead, it increases dramatically. Leadership roles change as the organization becomes more self-directed and self-managed, but the need for leadership is greater than ever. The paradox of leadership in the new organization is the more power a leader gives away, the more his or her leadership is required.

It is not always an easy concept to grasp. Most leaders have a difficult time adjusting, especially when it comes to letting go of their traditional spans of control. Knowing how much to relinquish can be confusing at times. One of our clients is a franchisee/franchisor organization that operates a number of restaurants for national chains. As this company started to change, the CEO began giving away all of his decision-making responsibilities, thinking that giving responsibility to people meant they should make all the decisions. He abdicated his decision-making entirely under this assumption. What he didn't realize was his role as leader still called for him to be a decision-maker. There are times when agreement can't be reached among teams, times when decisions must be made too quickly to build consensus, and times when executive decisions are necessary to ensure the organization moves forward.

The fact is, leaders are generally promoted because they maintain a positive vision, see the big picture, and think strategically. Most are good at what they do, which is making strategic decisions, choosing the right people for the right jobs, exhibiting vision, providing an example, coaching, teaching, and walking a fine line between chaos and control. Most companies enter into a period of chaos and confusion when a change effort is first introduced. That is when the leaders' ability to lead through vision becomes paramount.

"We had just a rough idea of where we were headed," said the COO of GOJO. "What kept us going forward was our vision of the future. We wanted to create an organization that was 'change-able.' We wanted GOJO to become a learning organization that embraced exploration of the new, created change from within, was innovative, and sought to improve continuously. Getting to that point, while trying to develop the strategies and tactics to keep the whole in balance and the individual parts moving in sync, was not easy. It was like building an airplane while in flight. It was leadership's responsibility to communicate a clear, future vision. Without vision to see you through, the change process would be impossible."

To enable the future vision of the company, leaders must constantly communicate it, while they maintain the Seven Conditions and Six Systems. As keepers of the culture, they must make vital decisions whenever necessary.

Part of the art of leadership is determining when decisions should be made through a team- or employee-based consensus, and when they must be made by leadership. We call this the "Noah Factor." Had Noah abdicated his decision-making role and waited to gain common ground with his peers before building the Ark, no creatures would have survived the flood. Noah knew "instinctively" (via revelation) that it was time for an executive decision, and he made what turned out to be an important move, all things considered. Within *The Whole Systems Approach*, most decisions are left to the work teams and employees; yet, during times when the work teams cannot find common ground or the "flood" is imminent, the leader must act. A critical ability is knowing which decisions to make and when.

The leader also plays a role of "contextualizer" by providing employees with a context or framework for their work. For example, if the company is trying to care better for its customers, leaders need to help employees see how their actions affect the company effort. Leaders also must become teachers, always alert for teaching moments during the work day. They must help people learn from their experiences so those experiences can be translated into positive action, the real manifestation of learning.

Leader actions have to match the rhetoric. Small things matter. For example, a CEO of a mid-sized manufacturing plant in the Midwest walked into an employee meeting recently and asked, "Where is our team-meeting agenda?"

"We don't have one," came a quiet reply. The employees watched nervously, wondering how the CEO would react. "Let's make one then," the CEO said with a shrug. He pulled a blank agenda form from his briefcase and spent the next few minutes working with the team designing the agenda. Ten minutes later, the agenda was done, and the meeting proceeded.

What was accomplished in this meeting was fairly routine; however, with one simple act, the drawing up of the agenda, the CEO had "walked his talk." He worked as an equal with the team, all the while reinforcing common language, practices, and values within the team. This not only helped solidify communication within the organization, it showed the team the importance of a simple tool like a meeting agenda. Word traveled throughout the organization that this was a CEO who backed up his rhetoric with action. He gained a good measure of credibility and trust by performing a task that took him no more than 10 minutes to complete.

How Decisions Are Made

A question that commonly arises is how decisions are to be made. In a living organization, there can be no "hard or fast" rule as to who makes which decisions, but there should be a clear framework. For an organization to have the flexibility and adaptability needed to thrive in the marketplace, decisions must be made on all levels. This doesn't mean anarchy. Leaders continue to make critical decisions. The shift is in the way leaders are legitimized. Decisions, not hierarchy, structure the way work is done and, therefore, become more important in the living organization, not less. The decision-making process generally follows three primary models: the emergent model, the consulted model, and the informed model.

The emergent model involves the "search for common ground." Emergent decisions occur when "common ground" agreements exist within the work team or group. These agreements emerge through discussion and a free flow of information. They surface when someone says, "I think we are 'good enough' to move forward on this." or "Wait a minute, we may have agreement here." The group then acknowledges that, in fact, a decision has been made; the decision is noted, and people move on.

In the consulted model, decisions are made by an identified decision-maker within the organization. This is usually the CEO, team leader, or another designated leader. The leader's actions during this process are crucial. He or she listens to everyone who needs or wants to act as a "consultant" on the decision. The leader then takes the information from the "consultants," and weighs it as part of the decision-making process. The decision is made by the leader or designated group alone, but once the decision is made, the leader is responsible to inform all involved of what the decision was, how it was made, and how their input was used.

The informed model is used mostly when a person or group receives up-front knowledge that others want simply to be informed. In this model, the group that made the decision will inform others that wish to be notified of the situation but who chose not to be active participants in the decision-making process. For example, some people may not care what brand of copy machine is purchased.

Decisions often bounce between these models. Emergent decisions are preferable whenever possible with consulted and informed decisions as fall-back models.

One CEO with whom we worked put a graphic exclamation point on the concept by standing in front of the 175 people in his organization wearing one hat and holding another. He wore a regular baseball cap, with the company's logo on it, when he was a participant in emergent decisions. Everyone in the room was given a similar hat at the beginning of the conference. It signified his voice was no more important than anyone else's in the room. He was just another voice in an emergent decision that required common ground.

On the other hand, when he put on his other hat—a large, red "Mad Hatter's" hat, this meant he was the decision-maker in a consulted decision. Pinned to the hat was an enormous set of plastic ears and lips. They signified that while he was to make the final decision himself, his responsibility was to listen to people before he made the decision, then report back to them as to what his decision was, why it was made, and how their consultation was considered.

While the outlandish hat helped relax everyone in the room, it worked to fully illustrate the decision-making process. During a three-day meeting, with all 175 employees involved, he wore his ball cap—his participant hat—98 percent of the time. Yet, when he put on his "Mad Hatter's" hat, people clearly understood and accepted the shift in his role.

A New Role for Managers

Middle managers have received the short end of the stick during the past 20 years, especially in change efforts involving reengineering and downsizing. It has almost become a fad to "fix" economic troubles within organizations by dumping managers. The future holds better news for managers as they learn to reinvent themselves while their organizations begin to appreciate the knowledge they bring to the table. The popular idea used to be that managers did not do any real work. Yet, many managers found themselves very dissatisfied. Once promoted to the management ranks because of their technical proficiency or their ability to be team players, managers often found themselves in lose-lose situations. They could no longer do the work they enjoyed and were good at doing and, therefore, slowly lost the respect of their fellow employees.

Microsoft's Bill Gates, in his book *The Road Ahead*, blamed many of IBM's struggles in the mid-1980s, when the giant firm lost its iron grip as the undisputed leader of the computer industry, on this role of managers. "IBM was such a great company," Gates noted. "Why did it have so much trouble with PC software development? One answer is that IBM tended to promote all of its good programmers into management."

In the past, the manager's job was to plan, control, direct, and evaluate. "Your job," they were told, "is to watch someone else work so you can direct what else needs to be done and evaluate whether the person doing the work is effective." Think for a moment about what that does to the person actually doing the work. As Peters said: "We've created organizations where adults must raise their hands to ask if they can go to the bathroom." It's obviously not a world of work where people are going to thrive. This old model did away with adult responsibility and trust to make decisions. We delegated the responsibility to managers, whose role it was to "control" and "evaluate" the employees. As a result, managers often incurred the wrath of employees and senior leadership alike.

Now, at the turn of the millennium, we walk in and tell managers they are suddenly obsolete. Watching someone else work is no longer a valid task. Organizations have shifted, but managerial roles have not. Managers have been left out in the cold because we haven't provided them with new skills or redefined the roles they play. We shifted, without allowing their role to shift also. Is it any wonder, then, why middle managers resist organizational change more than any other group? How can they get on board? They end up being impacted the most. We've taken their entire professional life away from them and told them they have no value. Yet, these are people with considerable skills, intellectual capital, and technical expertise. Rather than lose those valuable assets, leaders need to redefine the managers' roles and utilize their skills.

In many organizations, career paths are being developed in one of two ways: maturing managers become either technical experts or project leaders, mentors and coaches. This provides "managers" with an opportunity to do what Bill Gates suggests: go back to the technical skills that got them promoted to management in the first place and teach others, or develop skills that allow them to play the role of "tribal elders" in an organization. These tribal elders or "mentors" can facilitate growth in others while developing their own leadership talent. The role of manager has changed from one who watches and evaluates other people's work, to a technical contributor, coach, teacher, and project integrator. This not only ensures vital functions within the organization, it dramatically changes a manager's role from one that is perceived as negative to one that is positive. The traditional manager was too often seen as an adversary by employees because the manager watched and evaluated their work—a job that was ultimately demeaning to them both.

In the new organization, managers, as teachers and trainers, assist employees in managing themselves and their careers, enable results by breaking down barriers, and ensure inter/intra/integration between projects. This new role inspires trust between manager and employee. Managers are seen as fellow team players and helpers, rather than as adversaries. Mutual respect arises between employee and manager, rather than mutual suspicion. The benefit to the organization is enormous. Animosity between managers and employees, and between managers and senior leaders, is a major cancer that damages and even destroys relationships, communication, and, ultimately, results.

In the new paradigm of work, managers can play a wonderful and meaningful role in helping employees reach their potential, along with providing technical expertise. This is vastly different from their old role of watching another manager watch supervisors watching individuals who actually do the work. Managers may still carry out some traditional duties, depending on how the organization chooses to operate. In many cases, managers still evaluate the quality of work within teams and assume other responsibilities like firing and hiring, but this is done in cooperation with those teams and through tools such as feedback from peers, direct reports, and

leaders. The difference is in how people respond to being managed. If employees have a voice in the role "managers" play, they
are generally more open and supportive.

The Role of Employees

As employees become more experienced with and involved in
the change process, most decisions will be made where most of the
information resides—with the employee. Employees will make
most of the decisions that directly affect their work. This is a very
different model than the traditional command-and-control hierarchy where nearly all decisions are made at the top.

In the new paradigm of work, employees are accountable for
results, not the manager. They are required to think, make decisions,
and voice opinions. Employees become relationship builders and col-
laborators and develop broader, more cross-functional skills. As a
result, employees have more fun in these new roles because they are
more connected to the product or service they provide.

The following table reflects a high-level view of the shift
required in all roles.

New Roles

Who does what?	Before	During	After
Leader	Makes all strategic and many tactical decisions	Makes decisions with the organization	Organization and leaders both make decisions
	Commits to change	Demonstrates commitment	Continues to demonstrate commitment
	Directs employees; plans work; controls work and workers	Lets go of "control" Builds "broad base" of leadership	Assumes accountability for enterprise results versus tactical units
	Evaluates productivity	Sponsors teams; delegates sponsorship to others	Sponsors teams with other members

Leader (cont.)		Highly visible; models and reinforces	Ensures Seven Conditions for health
		Provides "big picture" context and ensures "meaning for change"	Continues to provide "big picture" context and direction
Manager	Watches/evaluates workers	Chooses path—technical contributor, coach or project lead	Moves to new role and no longer "watches" work
	Shuffles paper	Sponsors some teams	Continues to sponsor teams
	Controls budget, schedule, etc. for unit	Maintains aspects of traditional role, where necessary	Models use of the Accountability System and encourages others to do so
	Resolves problems	Shares in resolving problems with unit/team	Facilitates, coaches, leads
	Makes decisions for units	Lets go of "old baggage"	Shares decisions with unit/teams
	Voices ideas on behalf of employees	Voices own opinions/ideas and no longer serves as a "voice" for employees	
Sponsor	Usually doesn't exist; if it does, comes only from Senior Leader	Provides direction for team	Provides direction for team if needed
	Acts as "leader" for given team/project	Supports team leader	Ensures team vision is aligned to corporate initiatives
		Comes from formal/informal ranks	Comes from formal/informal ranks
		Facilitates as needed	Backs team play
		Develops team skills where needed	Inspires teamwork
		Eliminates obstacles and roadblocks	Eliminates roadblocks

Sponsor (cont.)			Acts as a guide—does not attend every meeting
Employees	Involved only in immediate work area	Encouraged to participate fully	Operate from a process-oriented, team-based view
	Usually follow orders from leaders	Actively voice ideas	Plan and control work
		Let "old baggage" go	Evaluate productivity
	Usually feel "less than" accountable, responsible or fully utilized	Make decisions with leadership about how the company will operate (all Alignment Model levels)	Act as decision-makers in all areas affecting work
			Adopt new behaviors/ competencies
			Accept personal responsibility and accountability

Honoring the Entire System

The Whole Systems Approach honors the system and the people in it by providing a world of work where people can stretch, thrive, and reach their full potential. The scope of personal change is enormous. People are required to let go of many of their old security blankets, including the tradition of fixed job descriptions, unchanging organization charts, defined spans of control, tight control, and autonomous decision-making.

Such a change requires long-term consistency, persistence, perseverance, and a strong belief and vision that it will lead to a better organization. People must accept the fact that the organization is a living system where everything doesn't always go as planned. Those courageous leaders who embrace *The Whole Systems Approach* will have a profound experience. One leader, Al Pino, COO of First Security Information Technology, Inc., observed, "I have never experienced anything that was so natural, tiring, rewarding, difficult, and energizing in my life. I feel very close to this work, and it has created many opportunities for me. I find satisfaction in knowing that I have experienced everything I have, expended everything I have, for the values I believe in. I've seen that it makes a difference in my life, in my family, with my closest friends, and with the people with whom I work." Pino likens himself to an elephant on an invisible chair. Once he let go of his limiting beliefs, new possibilities were evident in every area of his life.

In many ways, the stakes are raised, both personally and professionally. "My experiences and emotions since we began *The Whole Systems Approach* have run the gamut from extreme frustration to exhilaration," said MichCon's Ewing. "The frustrating part stems from the fact we are working against a moving standard under a clock that has only 24 hours a day. That is also what makes it so irresistible. It's that set of circumstances—the demand for excellence in a shorter period of time—that requires the best you have to offer. It is clearly the place I want to be."

Change—like most of the important things in life—requires a personal effort. A common theme among the thousands of senior leaders, managers, and employees we've worked with over the years is that whole systems change was the hardest thing they've ever done. But all of them have also told us they wouldn't trade the experience for anything.

If you think you can, or you think you can't, you're probably right!

—*Henry Ford*

Chapter

13

Personal
Alignment: Unleashing
the Power of Inherent
Potential

Organizations consist of individuals who represent a vast, untapped reservoir of hidden wealth. The personal and professional energy unleashed through *The Whole Systems Approach* can be incredible. However, the organization must coax that inherent potential—the unique capacity for greatness—to the surface, and then nurture it until it grows and flourishes. The challenge is to ensure the conditions and systems are in place to harness this tremendous power that lies dormant within the system.

Personal alignment is essential to unleashing inherent potential. People must change before the organization can. If people do not change, the possibilities of the organization achieving outstanding results are highly improbable. When employees realize a greater portion of their inherent potential, the company naturally enjoys the benefits of increased productivity while expanding the possibilities for breakthrough performance.

Achieving Personal Alignment

Personal alignment includes developing an awareness of your own belief systems and how your beliefs impact your actions and perceptions about the organization. This means owning the part you

185

have played in perpetuating the current culture. Personal alignment also involves achieving clarity regarding your own personal purpose, vision, and values for your life overall, not just your work life. This is a true process of self-discovery. The process of personal alignment requires calibration of the organization's purpose, vision, and values against your belief systems to determine where you are "out" of and where you are "in" alignment with the organization.

Additionally, personal alignment is about making the commitment to come into or improve on areas of alignment. This may mean that if it is truly not possible to achieve alignment where you are now, you make the decision to cycle out of the company or situation to another one where greater alignment is possible. Personal alignment means maintaining a continual openness to feedback, developing greater levels of self-awareness, and assuming 100 percent responsibility for the results you create, the actions you take, and the level at which you are contributing.

Developing Awareness

The adage that you can achieve only what you believe is a concept often used to underscore the importance of believing in yourself and in your vision and goals. But, it also works the other way around. Within many organizations, workers are indeed achieving what they believe, but what they believe are things like: "The bureaucracy within this organization makes it impossible for me to produce high-quality work. Management doesn't care about me. Work is supposed to be drudgery. I will be punished for taking risks. Supervisors and workers are my natural enemies. Senior leaders are to be feared. Senior leaders alone are responsible for the health of the company. The job of the boss is to boss others around. It isn't necessary or even desirable for me to know the organization's overall vision, purpose, or goals. My best day at work will be when I tell my boss where to stick the quarterly evaluation report. We are a mediocre company, and that's okay."

Most likely, one or two of these beliefs currently exist within your company. When employees or senior leaders espouse these beliefs, they become self-fulfilling prophesies. If most people believe the company is a certain way, then that is exactly the way the company is or remains. On the personal side, self-limiting beliefs are just as harmful. If you believe you cannot do a job, clearly you will not do that job well. If you feel you are a poor performer, you will most likely be one. These self-limiting beliefs are manifested in a lack of commitment, contribution, or performance. Negative attitudes and self-limiting beliefs remain perhaps the biggest problem within corporations today.

Negative belief systems affect performance. Negative belief systems also create obstacles to change. People naturally resist change—the unknown is always troubling and uncertain, but for those with little faith in themselves or the organization, change is even more difficult. During a corporate change effort, leaders typically declare, "We really want to hear what you think. You are our most important assets. We want to know how you feel. We want you to take responsibility for this change. And, we want you to take the risks."

These comments are likely to run up against each individual's experience with the company, and those experiences form their belief system. Changing this negative belief system is a critical step. New belief systems must be installed in place of self-limiting or negative ones. Beliefs are only thoughts, but they are the single greatest determinant for the outcomes that are perpetuated. The organization must arrive at the realization: "We have created and maintained these beliefs together, and we can also change them to foster the culture we really want to exemplify."

The Buck Stops Here

Few employees will change their beliefs for long unless they begin to see a change within leadership. It just won't happen any other way. Leadership must blaze the trail for others to follow. Leaders can build trust and enhance credibility by providing the example and the model. Today leaders must challenge their perceptions of employees in their organizations. When MichCon was in the process of changing their culture, CEO Ewing observed, "An initial change for us was for leaders to let go of the old idea that people needed to be told what to do, and they must be constantly watched to see whether they would do it. Our leaders had to grasp the reality that employees are responsible adults who can run their own lives and contribute to a broader enterprise."

Ewing further noted, "We had to move away from the old notion of a manager as the controller of information, resources, scheduling, and so forth. We had to move toward a new image of a manager as someone between a leader and a coach. The new manager had to take on the responsibility for maintaining a healthy work environment and ensuring that the best workforce brought to the party is the one that consistently attends—and making awards based upon contributions. What was needed was a change of beliefs and a new set of skills."

Like Ewing, leaders must be willing to show others how to discard old beliefs and test assumptions by modeling new ones through their actions and behaviors. For example, in many companies, employees hold the belief that in spite of the espoused "open-door" policy, management really doesn't care what employees think. Will this change because management announces a "new-and-improved" open door policy? Of course not. Employees, most of whom are skeptical if not downright cynical, require more than rhetoric to change their beliefs.

Leaders and managers must show they have changed their own beliefs through their actions and behaviors. Only through direct action can leaders prove they have not only adopted a new belief but have acted on it consistently. The actions of these role models are critical. Without leaders out in front of the pack, organizations have little chance of shedding their limiting belief systems.

We were in a meeting not long ago with the CEO of a billion-dollar corporation and seven of his direct reports. Over many months, this CEO had been working with his direct reports and several other managers in an effort to open up the lines of communication throughout the company. Things were not going well, and the CEO was frustrated by the lack of results.

On a break, he shared his frustration with us by saying, "I think I'm going crazy here. All my managers want to do is sit around and talk about how incompetent their teams are. It's pathetic. They aren't taking on any responsibility. Nobody trusts anybody around here. Some of these guys actually hide out whenever any member of the leadership team comes their way. How can they expect to get anything done with that attitude? What am I going to do?"

There was no easy way to tell him that the change had to start, not with them, but with him. The truth was, he was a major part of the problem. His direct reports were modeling his behavior 100 percent down the line. He was often intolerant and highly critical of them, and they, in turn, were highly critical of their own teams. He criticized them for hiding out in their offices when things got tough, but, of course, that was exactly what he was doing. He hoarded information, failed to have a direct line-of-sight to the customer, and raised office politics to a highly developed art form. He was an excellent role model and an excellent teacher, but he was modeling and teaching the wrong things! His organization mirrored his personal misalignment.

To his credit, when we began to coach him, he became aware of the outcomes of his behavior. He took it upon himself to change his own behavior and bring himself into personal alignment with the goals he had expressed for the company. People noticed the change immediately, but it took a little time before they were convinced the change was for real. Once they were convinced, though, changes began to take place throughout the entire company. Managers came out of their offices during crises and followed the CEO's new example of confronting problems head-on. Communication became a commodity available to everyone, and the organization's productivity made a noticeable recovery.

Achieving Clarity

Unleashing inherent potential and modeling personal alignment creates the environment for breakthrough performance. Individuals need to personally experience the same process the organization goes through to create alignment, beginning with a clarification of personal purpose, vision, and values.

Breakthrough Performance

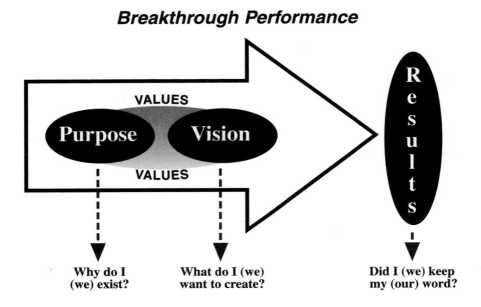

Articulating personal purpose and vision is often one of the most exciting, meaningful, frightening, and powerful experiences for an individual. If people are given the opportunity to explore their purpose—from both a functional and a personal perspective—they are more likely to envision a compelling future. For many, clarifying personal purpose and vision marks the first time in their lives they have considered these issues in depth. The clarification process can launch a voyage of self-discovery and provide baseline data that can then be used as an overlay to the organization's own purpose and values.

Why Do I Exist?

When working on aligning individuals, the first thing we explore is the question of personal purpose. We begin the process by asking each individual to develop something like a personal mission statement, then take it a step further and draw a distinction between their functional purpose and their personal purpose. For example, as parents, our functional purpose is to provide food, clothing, and shelter for our children. Our higher, more personal purpose is to ensure our children are successful in the world and in their personal lives. We endeavor to instill in them the values that will allow them to grow and realize as much of their personal potential as possible.

An individual's functional purpose (what I do) is based on activities, tasks, skills. An individual's personal purpose (why I exist) is about creating a meaningful existence, making a difference, leaving a legacy, increasing the sphere of influence, and tapping into a source of energy that is compelling and engaging. Both purposes are critical, but they are fundamentally distinct. In most corporations, employees are sometimes asked to focus on their functional purpose, but rarely is the personal, higher purpose ever broached by management. Thus, most corporations are badly out of alignment with the inherent potential of their employees, and, therefore, the inherent potential of the organization.

When we introduced this exploration of individual purpose at MichCon, some surprising and satisfying answers emerged. Employees, through a series of lively and animated discussions, determined their functional purpose was tied directly to their specific jobs. For secretaries, it was to provide administrative support so communications didn't break down; for field service employees, it was to provide high-level maintenance on the reliability of gas flow; and for salespeople, it was to reach as many potential customers as possible with information about the company so they could choose MichCon as their energy provider. Each individual had a different functional purpose, but they understood clearly how that purpose was tied to the overall vision of the company and its higher purpose.

What was MichCon's higher purpose? Every employee in MichCon had a hand in providing a vital service to hundreds of thousands of people who relied on that service not only for crucial daily needs but often for their very lives. For example, if the company didn't provide natural gas on time in the middle of a Michigan winter, people's lives would be placed in peril. Minimally, customers would suffer hardships and stress.

Breakthrough Performance

A Purpose Statement	Elements of a Purpose Statement
• Last a lifetime	• What activities/roles do I find fulfilling?
• Is bigger than I am	• What is the compelling motivation behind those activities/roles?
• Points me toward action	• What are my unique qualities and characteristics?
• Permits me to reach out and influence others	• What are the areas/qualities of the optimal environment I want to create around myself?

After each person has identified his or her personal purpose, he or she then describes the personal purpose in front of team members and explains how it connects to those of their team and the company. This sharing and disclosure are best facilitated by someone who will create a safe environment, given the personal risk involved in self-disclosing. People are often shy at first; however, once the process starts rolling, it usually becomes extremely meaningful. People share things with each other that they've never shared before.

For example, one man talked about his family for the first time in 27 years on the job. Prior to this time, he held the belief that families and business don't mix. As a consequence of his perception, he only brought his "work self" to the organization, leaving the best part of him at the door. As it turned out, he loved talking about his family. For the first time in his life, he felt "whole" at work. Sharing his personal life with his colleagues gave him a sense of community at work he had never experienced before.

Some people naturally fear such disclosure and close off to the process. That's why we offer it as a choice; participation isn't mandatory. But, we find that nearly everyone ultimately participates, once they feel safe to do so. While many people make real strides in personal growth, this powerful exercise nearly always builds community within the organization as well. The process of defining personal purposes is an overwhelmingly positive one, and people come out of this experience feeling closer and safer with each other.

The process also helps people make a direct connection between what they do on a day-to-day basis and a higher purpose in their lives. For example, at GOJO, the organization's purpose is, "Well-being through healthy skin." While making various skin care products may be an employee's functional purpose, helping other people gain well-being reflects the higher purpose of their work. It makes what they do matter. While they may spend their lives filling soap bottles, they come to realize their work is ultimately connected to improving the lives of hundreds of thousands of their customers. That's why the company's direct connection and vision to its customers is so important. This higher purpose work exists in all organizations, but it must be clearly defined and connected to the functional work that people do.

What Do I Want to Create?

As part of this process, employees define their life's vision and identify their core values. Vision is a declaration of a compelling future individuals are committed to creating for themselves. During the process, an open and full dialogue usually occurs. Clarifying our purpose and vision helps shape our attitudes, how we want to be viewed from the outside, and how we want to feel after working on the inside.

This exercise allows them to explore their own motivations and desires. They emerge with a deep understanding of what they want and need to feel optimistic and fulfilled.

Calibrating Organizational and Personal Alignment

Once personal vision is clarified, participants compare their personal purposes and visions to those of the organization. People quickly see where things are in or out of alignment. Are they using their purpose and vision to drive their activities and contributions to the organization? Are the organization's activities and contributions in alignment with their personal purpose and vision? The answers are extremely important. Only when the highest and best use of each individual is being manifested can the full potential of that person and, subsequently, of the organization be realized.

We ask some tough questions: "Are my personal purpose and values in alignment with those of the organization?" And, if not, "Why not? Where are we out of sync?" And, most important, "Once we have diagnosed a misalignment problem, how do we move into alignment even one more notch?" Interestingly enough, some who have declared themselves out of alignment have made the decision to leave the company and find a place where they can feel more aligned. Others have committed to come into full alignment and, many times, become the company's most loyal allies. Either way, it is a choice based on awareness that is critical for all employees to make.

It is important to note here that alignment is not an end state. All of us move in and out of alignment throughout our lives. It isn't a judgment as in "the jury is in". There is no "good or bad, right or wrong" attached. It is simply a matter of careful monitoring and diagnosing when you, as an employee or a colleague, are out of alignment. It is about awareness, not judgment. The only time misalignment becomes a "bad" thing is when it has not been diagnosed or is left untreated over time. When this occurs, disease sets in, leading to cynicism, lack of motivation, damaged relationships, and poor productivity. Another symptom of misalignment is when you continually go home after work feeling listless, unmotivated, and even angry. Something is definitely out of whack! This is not the way it has to be. It is time to reexamine your situation and ask, "Where am I out of alignment? Do I want to stay there? What can I do to be in sync?"

Creating personal and professional alignment generates enormous positive energy. Misalignment sets up a situation analogous to four people trying to push a stalled car but getting nowhere because they are all pushing in different directions. This alignment of purpose and vision allows everyone to push in the same direction. Which illustration best describes your work life? In which environment are you more likely to be productive?

This personal alignment of purpose and vision is not necessary for the survival of the organization. Many companies today are sur-

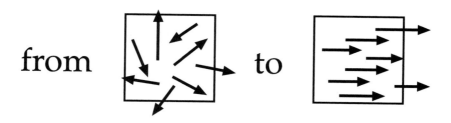

from   to

viving with employees and managers whose personal values, purpose, and vision are diametrically opposed to those of the company. Many others have only partial alignment within their ranks, and continue to pull down profits. Yet, while companies can survive with an indifferent and even cynical workforce, they cannot thrive! They cannot maximize their profits over the long term. Worse, they may face serious problems in the future as increased technology and global competition place additional stress on their unhealthy internal systems. Only when people are working with the same focus, broad as it may be, and are inspired in their workplaces will maximum productivity be achieved.

Dimensions of Alignment

Personal alignment is the cornerstone of the entire effort. For the organization, creating the environment where each employee, manager, and leader is encouraged to help develop and come into personal alignment with the values, purpose, and vision of the organization is essential to unleashing inherent potential and manifesting quantum results. Some dimensions of alignment include knowing specifically and positively what you want, participating 100 percent, being willing to work outside your comfort zone and to tell the truth to yourself and others, behaving as if you own the business, working for others' benefit, owning your results, doing whatever it takes, and allowing others to see and know who you are.

In one exercise, we ask people to list all the things they've chosen not to be responsible for in their lives. Few, of course, write down anything. Then we suggest they write, on the other side of the paper, all the things for which they choose to be responsible. Then, a designated partner conducts a reality check for them. The partner writes down a perception of that person. "What you must realize," we say, "is that for everything written on this side of the paper, you can no longer claim that you're a victim. You can't be a victim if you are responsible for these things."

Then we encourage people to tell stories of times when they chose not to be victimized by either the people or the events in their lives. At this point, it no longer seems heroic to be a victim; rather, the opposite is true. Some have learned this concept long before. But, for most people, the exercise has a powerful message: If we come from a place where we are 100 percent responsible for what happens in our lives, we can no longer live in or encourage "victimhood."

Committing to Improvement: Types of Contributions

At their highest level, our actions within the workplace can be seen in terms of whether or not we keep our word. Ultimately, keeping our word is about the contributions we make to our team and the organization. There are three levels of contributions: irrelevant, detrimental, or instrumental. Obviously, in two of these cases, we are not keeping our word.

In any situation, our contribution is being evaluated by ourselves and our peers. These contributions can be irrelevant, meaning we just take up space; detrimental, meaning we obstruct efforts by others to resolve the problem and perhaps cause additional problems; or instrumental, meaning whatever is achieved would not be as good without our meaningful contribution.

If our contribution is either irrelevant or detrimental, we are replaceable! Consider that 0 percent of a wonderful thing is nothing: The organization simply doesn't need us if we contribute at this level. Any self-evaluation should include the question, "Is what I am doing instrumental to achieving the established goal?" If not, it's time to rethink your position and choose to contribute in a different way.

This framework can be placed around every action we take or don't take within an organization. If we take 100 percent responsibility for our results and choose to make instrumental contributions to our professional and personal lives, we will be positive forces for change. If we come to work and gather around the coffee maker with other victims, sharing our victim stories, blaming others, rejecting self-examination and making ourselves right, then we have made a choice to either maintain the status quo or even make it worse. We have chosen to make irrelevant or detrimental contributions. As a result, we have no right to say this culture, which we profess to hate and blame for our problems, isn't our responsibility. If we do nothing to change it, then we are sustaining it.

To make an instrumental contribution, we need to say, "You know what, I'm not going to keep that detrimental culture alive today. I'm not going to hang out with the same old gang today. And when I hear a victim story, I'm not going to honor it. Instead, I'm going to suggest that instead of complaining, we should spend our energy coming up with solutions."

Of course, this isn't always easy. When we take this bold route, we risk alienating the people who live in victimhood, because they will likely be offended by our lack of sympathy. But, we have to ask, "What contribution have they made to my life and work?" We may find that they have been making a detrimental contribution for as long as we have chosen to associate with them. Victimhood is like a drug; it may makes us feel good in the short term, but the long-term price we pay is high. Kicking the addiction requires personal strength and courage. But, breaking free and growing again is the only route, once you realize the personal and professional rewards you reap for accepting full responsibility for your actions, choices and contributions are limitless.

Making this change doesn't happen without some serious effort. Having conducted hundreds of personal development workshops, we have witnessed many people struggle, initially, with this shift. To help, we conduct an exercise in our workshops. We divide people seated in the front of the room into three sections, each relating to one of the three types of contributions. We ask the entire organization to put themselves into one of the three groups. Do they consider their contributions to be irrelevant, detrimental, or instrumental? The vast majority place themselves in the instrumental grouping. However, when they are asked how they think their customers see the organization's contributions as a whole, many of them choose the other two categories. In other words, most don't think much of the contributions of their peers or supervisors. While they see their own contributions as worthy, they view the overall effort by the organization as lacking. It's always the "other guy" who is messing up.

In the 15 years we've conducted this exercise, this has happened every single time! People rate themselves as effective, but the organization as ineffective. They don't take responsibility for being the organization. The exercise often serves as a catharsis for managers and employees alike. They see clearly that they are not aligned with the organization and are not taking responsibility for being a part of the organization. It leads to some wonderful conversations where people say things like: "Hey, maybe we're not being accountable here. Let's do something about it." That something often brings hundreds of people into alignment individually and with the organization for the first time in their careers.

The aftermath of investing the time and energy for organization members to discover themselves through the personal alignment process is often defined by discovery, excitement, and renewed commitment. "It's changed my life" is a statement we've heard hundreds of times during and after these workshops. "I've not only become a better worker and leader, but a better spouse, parent, and friend. Not only that, I've regained confidence in the organization. The company didn't just invest in itself this time. It invested in me and in my life."

The intent behind personal alignment is to give everyone an opportunity to align with the organization and also to develop themselves. Realistically, not everyone will welcome this challenge. But, 100 percent alignment isn't necessary for your company to make significant strides. Most companies have results similar to these. One CEO says: "I estimate about 20 percent of our employees really jumped into the deep end of this process right away. They were the ones who took the whole nine yards, including the personal alignment and full accountability. Most employees and managers remained in the middle—they embraced the change in some ways, and held back in others. As a group, they are slowly moving to embrace the changes, but they are more cautious than the first group. A small percentage rejected the process out of hand. That's worked out okay because most of them self-selected out of the company. We haven't had to ask many to leave. The important thing, though, is that these percentages are more than enough already to make it worthwhile."

Along with clarifying purpose and vision, a well-defined sense of community and connectivity develops through this personal alignment process. People begin to realize they can "wholly" contribute in this organization—connected to themselves, their work, the people with whom they work, the industry, and the customers they serve. Set aside is the old notion that you must park your personal self at the door whenever you enter the professional workplace. Many progressive companies have come to this conclusion. IBM, for example, recently did away with its nepotism policy because IBM leadership recognized that many people were meeting and falling in love at work. Previously, one of the employees would have to quit if they married another employee. "Who are we kidding?" IBM management said. "This is where people spend most of their waking hours. Of course they are going to meet and form strong relationships. After all, isn't that what we want them to do?"

Ongoing Self and Community Assessment

One way to determine whether your purpose and vision are in alignment with those of the organization is by taking a close look at the results you are producing. Results are about keeping your word—do you do what you say you will do? These results will often tell you whether you are being true to your purpose and vision. For example, one CEO we worked with wrote that one of his goals was to bring "on-time quality to every activity and product" he delivered. For more than a year, the company struggled to meet that goal. We were asked to intervene. One of the first things we observed was the CEO arrived consistently late to meetings, a fact that diminished not only his effectiveness but also his credibility with his managers. He was not "walking his talk" by backing up his purpose and values with action. As a result, the company, too, was lax and late, and the on-time quality suffered. Results are the barometer that show clearly whether you are in or out of alignment.

A Community of Truth

Self-awareness helps minimize the time we are out of alignment, but on occasion it still occurs, often without us realizing it. That's why employees, managers, and senior leaders need to help coach each other.

CINDY: Last summer I took water skiing lessons. I felt comfortable with my skills, but my coach challenged me by saying I was holding back. "But I'm not," I insisted. "You are," my coach countered. "You're holding back. You think you're feeling it, but trust me, you're not."

He showed me how to move my body into a slightly different position—a change of about four inches. I was amazed at the difference. That tiny move allowed my weight to become aligned with the ski. Instead of fighting the physical forces involved, I was suddenly able to utilize them. Just a small change gave me far better results without adding to the amount of energy I was expending. In fact, it released energy I did not realize I had.

Often, people in organizations make the mistake of thinking it is going to take a Titanic effort to get into alignment, when often it requires only one small move to utilize their energy more fully. We all have "blind spots" that can be detected by a good coach, friend, or mentor. The first step toward self-awareness is to gather a team of people around you who will give you accurate and honest feedback regarding how you relate to people and your alignment in general. Most of us—especially senior leaders—think we are in alignment, but are sheltered from the truth because those around us are not conditioned to tell us the truth. Most people in organizations circle one another as if they were part of a self-contained solar system, rarely daring to help each other by sharing an observation that might be construed as critical.

BILL: During coaching sessions, I always ask this question: "Do you have at least one person who regularly gives you honest, trusted information about how you are impacting others?" The answers are always revealing. Most senior leaders admit they don't even have one person providing this vital information, let alone an entire community. In most corporate cultures, we cut off all this tremendously valuable insight that others can provide.

Everyone must play critical roles to build a safe community within the organization where such information can be shared in a trusting atmosphere. Part of the trust comes from the frequent articulation by leadership that this feedback is important and should be given and received in a spirit of cooperation and support. The questions become, "How many of you want to be the only ones who don't know you are ineffective in a certain area? How many of you don't want to know how you are impacting the performance of others?" While there may, in fact, be a few who truly do not want this information, we have found that most people do. This requires building in performance feedback as an informal as well as formal part of the culture.

Feedback as "A Gift"

One characteristic of a high-performance organization is "ongoing performance feedback." We all have a basic human need to know how we are viewed by those around us in our personal and professional lives. For feedback to be considered a gift, it must come in the form of positive feedback (what I want you to continue or what I appreciate) and improvement feedback (to be more effective, consider doing more of, less of, stop doing, or start doing). If people feel they are valued and respected, then the spirit of solidarity and cooperation can grow quite strong. In organizations where people operate from their own agendas with little trust, people feel vulnerable and are less likely to solicit or accept constructive criticisms about alignment or anything else for that matter.

Throughout this process, the relationships you develop will define just how far you can go. Everything comes through relationships. People should be encouraged to ask: "What relationships have I developed and nurtured within this company? When someone has something difficult to tell me that may just save me in a given situation, will they do it? Am I self-aware enough to understand how valuable these relationships are such that when someone comes in and provides information about me that is important (even if it is temporarily painful to hear), I will listen versus biting his or her head off?" A direct relationship exists between how self-aware we are and our effectiveness.

Although many people are afraid of feedback because it has always been a negative experience for them, a safe environment can be created for teams and the organization. In fact, with time and experience, people not only don't fear feedback, but actively seek it. Feedback must shift from "leveling somebody" to "leveling with somebody."

Recently, we worked with the senior leaders of a worldwide insurance company. One of the first things we did at the session was hand out copies of the parable *The Emperor's New Clothes*. At first, we received a number of blank stares. "Why *The Emperor's New Clothes*?" one person finally asked. "Because, like the Emperor, most of you have no idea what impact you are having on the people around you, including your customers, because no one will tell you the truth!" we answered. Not only had they cut themselves off from any feedback from their employees and other managers, they had no idea of the potential impact of their plans for a massive change effort. This lack of awareness made it highly unlikely their effort would succeed.

Assuming Responsibility: Who is responsible for our choices?

As adults, we all choose our situations, whatever they are—our jobs, our family lives, our economic status, and every other thing that makes up our existence. We make these choices everyday. We either make decisions by default, by not doing anything at all, or through active choices. Either way, we are responsible. An ongoing choice we can always make is to be a victim. If we work with a colleague who is not doing his or her job, and we choose not to say anything about it, then we need to be responsible for the fact we chose not to act. If we see someone steal something at work or a person misrepresent a situation and we do nothing, we make a choice that perpetuates the problem. We are culpable and accountable for the ramifications. These are critical concepts for everyone to grasp and accept. We are all 100 percent responsible for our actions (or inactions) 100 percent of the time—and we have the freedom of choice. These two concepts alone can turn organizations into highly productive and thriving operations!

100 Percent Personal Responsibility

The foundation of personal alignment is personal responsibility. Taking full responsibility for your actions is one of the highest forms of human maturity and one of the toughest things to master. For example, how many times have you run into a situation like this: It's trash pickup day, and you say to your 13-year-old, "Make sure you take the garbage out this morning." Your 13-year-old responds with: "Sure, Dad, I will try!" That afternoon you return home, and what is sitting near the garage door? The still-full garbage can, of course. "What happened to the garbage? Why didn't you take it out like I asked?" you thunder at your teenager, who is lying on the couch finishing off a bag of your favorite potato chips.

Is your child's response likely to be, "Oh, I'm very sorry. I messed up. I'm 100 percent responsible for not doing what you asked. I won't ever make that mistake again." Or, are you likely to hear a stream of excuses, reasons, and stories about why the garbage isn't out?

We are, it seems, hard-wired from an early age to come up with these "reasons, stories, or excuses." Later in life, we add BMW (bitching, moaning, and whining) to the "reasons, stories, or excuses" to complete a total package of irresponsibility.

The fact is, however, you either have "reasons, stories, or excuses" or you have "results." You can't have both.

Our own responsibility is to stay in alignment as much as possible. Our ability to take responsibility—and to accept when we are out of alignment without the "reasons, stories, or excuses" and BMW—is critical to this process. In fact, we've found that using the terminology of "reasons, stories, or excuses" and BMW in a playful way is of great value in most corporations. It helps create a common, non-threatening language that helps build a set of shared beliefs and values.

Reasons vs. Results

- Working or Not
- Account for
- Ownership
- Learning

- Total Responsibility
- Commitment
- Results

- Right or Wrong
- Blame
- Collusion
- Victim

- Reasons
- Stories
- Excuses

Vision/Resistance/Maintenance

Alignment is sustained only when we come from a position of personal responsibility and accountability. Any number of activities can motivate and excite people about getting into alignment, but to maintain that momentum over months and years, employees must be willing to accept personal responsibility for their own choices. Victims typically come from a place of blame. All failures or setbacks they suffer are blamed on the organization or specific colleagues or supervisors. Victims also come from a place of always being right. They rarely, if ever, admit culpability, and they always have their "story" about their victimization. They often spend a great deal of time and effort telling their "victim's tale" to other people, who are usually other self-styled victims. Together, they commiserate about how miserably they have been treated and how it wasn't their fault.

Those who come from a position of responsibility, however, focus on the end result that will tell them whether they succeeded in reaching their goals. They accept responsibility in either case—whether they reached their goal or not. People coming from a frame of responsibility openly admit their mistakes and then learn from them. This all becomes part of a process that sooner or later yields high productivity and success. Victims deny mistakes and thus deny themselves the chance to learn from their mistakes. When nothing is learned from a mistake, it quickly evolves into something much more troublesome. A mistake that produces a lesson is a temporary setback that may even have hidden payoffs. A mistake with no lesson attached is the definition of a real failure.

In one exercise, we ask participants to pair up with someone else and share their "victim's story," if they have one. Most people have one or more, and many people become quite animated as they relate the story of how they were "done wrong." After everyone is finished venting and telling their stories, we pause for a moment, then ask them to tell their stories again. This time, though, they have to tell the story from an accountable point of view. They have to point out where they made choices along the way, and where they might have avoided being "victimized." Many people can identify two or more key choices they made along the way that led to the disastrous consequence.

It's an eye-opening exercise, and those with open minds begin to realize their own choices played a major role in whatever occurred. They come to see that while telling their victim's story is easy and they experience a satisfying self-righteousness, deep down, it isn't an entirely honest story. As good as it feels, it becomes clear there is a heavy price for telling such stories. It starts an erosion of self-respect that, left unchecked, can do serious damage. It also affects their relationships with other "victims," because those who take responsibility for their actions have little patience with "victimitis."

At the same time, there are moments when we are all true victims, when disaster occurs through no fault of our own. But, there is a major difference between being a victim and living in "victimhood." In too many organizations, people are living in victimhood. Some have lived there all their adult lives. These people spin stories of victimization around the water cooler, lunch table, or over drinks after work and encourage others to do the same. This constitutes an exceedingly negative and counterproductive attitude that undermines morale and productivity. Yet, many organizations not only tolerate this attitude from employees, their unhealthy internal culture actually fosters this cult of victimhood.

In one such IS organization, they had perpetuated victimhood so much they truly believed they were at "the bottom of the food chain." Imagine going to work every day knowing that you would be blamed for something you felt you had no control over. Imagine feeling that no matter what you did, you would be disregarded, disrespected, and end up "the fool" regardless. This is how this entity felt! It wasn't until the members of IS realized that they had unconsciously shifted over the years from "victim" to "victimhood" that they could begin making the small shifts required to gain self-respect and eventually earn the respect of the organization.

These people were not bad people. They needed the awareness and the tools to start taking pride in their work lives. This is why paying attention to organizational self-esteem is so vital. Where you see low morale or "victim talk," you know people have lost something they value. To organizations, this lost self-esteem—pride and confidence—equates to lost time and low levels of productivity. The goal of every organization can be to build a corporate environment where 100 percent of the people take 100 percent responsibility for their actions 100 percent of the time. Along with this goes the caveat that these same employees, who are unafraid to admit their mistakes, learn from them and do not make the same ones over and over again. This organization has the opportunity to become a continual learning organization. It's a much healthier and honest place to work.

Personal responsibility is an attitude that transcends the workplace, once it is instilled and supported by the work culture. People realize that taking 100 percent responsibility for what they do in their lives is not only a liberating attitude, it is an empowering one as well. Once people begin to take responsibility for their lives and their choices, they find it is nearly impossible to retreat back to victimhood. Leaders can play a huge part in building this culture of self-responsibility by taking the "blame" out of things. If blame, guilt, and finger-pointing are popular games people play within the organization, then few people will respond to a call for accountability.

Accountability and responsibility must be rewarded at all times, and victimhood stories must be labeled as such and addressed before any cultural shift will occur internally. This is especially true in situations where an honest mistake has been made. These events are valuable teaching moments. People are usually outside their comfort zones when confronting their own mistakes. Everyone should recognize this and make sure—without blame and chastisement—the correct lesson is learned so the mistake doesn't occur again. In a blame-free environment, people are more open right after they make a mistake. A successful leader will seize the moment as learning from mistakes facilitates the achievement of results—the "proof is in the pudding."

The pathway to change set forth in *The Whole Systems Approach* is anything but easy. We haven't set out the gear for climbing a hill—or even a mountain, for that matter. This process is for climbing the mountain—the Mt. Everest of corporate change.

Results: The Return on Investment

There is nothing easy about this challenge. At one point or another, you will find yourself in thin air indeed, and the summit may even be obscured from view. From time to time, the oxygen may become precious and the temperatures bone-chilling, and the whole thing may not seem worth it. You may be tempted to throw off the attempt and flee back down to the safety of what you left far below. And, why not? All you will miss is a chance to see the view from the top.

But, before you take on this ultimate challenge, you might determine what the returns will be for embarking on such an adventure. The ROI (Return On Investment) is the engine that drives *The Whole Systems Approach*. This approach was designed specifically to leverage the investment in time and resources and to contribute to building a cohesive whole. The process requires energy and commitment, but the results—given a persistent and consistent effort by leadership and the organization—provide a staggering, long-term yield.

Through *The Whole Systems Approach*, an organization can truly transform itself, and at the same time, acquire the competency for continual change and reconfiguration. One of the substantive advantages of gaining the "view from the top" through this process is what you learn along the way. Specifically, the organization becomes highly capable of rapid change—change-able. With an aligned, motivated, creative, and responsible workforce, several competitive advantages emerge. For example, companies investing in this approach have achieved some impressive results, including accomplishing successful, fundamental change and corporate reinvention, accelerating the speed of traditional change by a multiple of four, creating organization-wide ownership of the effort by all stakeholders, producing outstanding results that could not have been accomplished using traditional approaches, and developing self-reliance for sustaining a thriving organization. Companies have also achieved stakeholder involvement, alignment, commitment, dramatically improved results, and an environment where people thrive while creating a resilient and flexible organization that is well positioned for success.

Three Living Examples

The following three examples are representative of the results gained by scores of leaders and organizations.

1. FSITI: Finding Real Success

When FSITI started with this approach, they were struggling unsuccessfully with a change effort, which was not Mt. Everest, yet they couldn't see their way to the top. Change was imperative because FSITI's parent company was completely dissatisfied with the results they were getting. As the leadership team began to establish the parameters for the effort, they agreed the change needed to be sweeping and involve the whole system.

The company, through a total involvement strategy, initiated massive, radical change in process, structure, and competencies. In the space of 24 months, the organization shifted from failing their customer to succeeding. Al Pino, president of FSITI, helped spearhead the entire change effort and lead the ascent up the mountain. "The large group conferencing process is the fastest way to focus a company to a common vision," he said. "If any business person can't get excited about that prospect, they should check for a pulse."

Project manager Karen Wardle also has a keen appreciation both for the challenges of the climb, and for the view from the top. "Looking back at the initial resistance to change makes me realize how far we've come," she said. "We are not only talking about a conservative financial institution, we are also in the high-tech section. We were trying to change a culture of banking nerds. It was wildly optimistic to think we could do that. We were in a rowboat chasing Moby Dick, but we had the tartar sauce just in case."

FSITI went through the process and momentum began to take hold. "There was this amazing creativity and brainstorming," Wardle said. "What we scarcely realized was that the process was creating new structure within the company. The timeframes, the teambuilding, the participation of everyone in the organization—we were changing as we went into action without being aware of it. It was such a natural process. By that I don't mean it was easy. All of us went to hell and back together. We yelled together, cried together, pulled out our hair together, and felt triumphant together at times, too. All the methodologies, from the process mapping to the agenda making, became part of the way we did things, and soon the organization embraced them as its own. Today, large group conferencing is a natural process within the organization, and so is the whole systems method of thinking. It is embedded in the culture—from the top echelon of leadership to the part-time guy on the graveyard shift whose name few people know."

Wardle witnessed a complete transformation within the company. "Our work product got out the door faster, the quality improved dramatically, and, most importantly, the parent company is thrilled with the change—in no small way because they can see the systems are in place for the company to continually improve into the future."

If the parent company had any doubts as to the results from the change process, their doubts were laid to rest not long ago when three of the six mainframe processors at FSITI crashed the week before Columbus Day. The entire company faced an unmitigated disaster. Banks cannot be closed and customers cannot be kept from their money, so the loss of the computer functions put the company in an impossible situation. Under normal circumstances in a traditional organizational structure, the estimated time to a full recovery would have been from six months to a year. Luckily, the new organization process had already taken hold inside the company and a team of people—none of whom had titles and none of whom cared about titles—attacked the problem.

"They made a commitment that they would be operational the Sunday before Columbus Day—get everything back on line within 92 hours," said Wardle. "No one believed them. But, they cut through all the red tape and did things their own way. They solved problem after problem with incredibly creative solutions because they were not only free to do so, they were encouraged to think for themselves. They had only one focus—to resolve the problem. No energy, time, or resource was expended on getting things approved or developing a plan that had to be approved by management. There was such tremendous trust between each team member at every level that they could do the job, and they pulled it off. They met their deadline and had everything back and running within four days. Four days! It was totally amazing. If we hadn't gone through transformation, we could never have done it. I guess we caught that whale with our rowboat after all."

The project could not be accomplished without the foundation having been established for working together—stripping away the politics and surrendering the egos. FSITI began by coordinating a large group conference that was open to anyone in the organization who wished to attend. The purpose of the conference was to declare a disaster, establish a mission, identify goals, determine roles, explore options, and align the rest of the organization so everyone was excited about being a part of the solution.

During those 92 hours, FSITI pulled off miracle after miracle, from deciding whether to repair, replace, or upgrade the system to building a whole new room and installing a completely new system. Contractors were literally laying the last pieces of the floor as the machine was being rolled in.

After the project was completed, one vendor observed that he had never seen such a diverse group of people come to consensus within three hours and walk out supporting that decision. He was amazed that during the project, no one was needed to mediate, and there was no dissension or negative discussion. This would not have been possible if the trust did not already exist and the people had not been confident in their ability to work together. Al Pino noted that it would have been impossible to achieve what they achieved if they had not engaged the whole system in the process.

For Wardle and most leaders we work with, the positive results from the process aren't limited to the product and organization. "From a personal standpoint, *The Whole Systems Approach* brought about tremendous changes for me," Wardle said. "I had spent my life in companies thinking, 'Why don't they listen? I know how to do this! I'm valuable, I'm trained. I know how this works! Like most employees and leaders around me, I felt free to criticize the company because I felt I was speaking from outside the 'inner circle.' After this process took hold, I was—for the first time in my career—put in a position of total responsibility. I'd say, 'I'm valuable, I'm trained,' and suddenly a group of people would say: 'Okay, Karen, go for it. It's all yours. Make it work.' It's scary because suddenly you realize your job is on the line. You begin to tremble a little. Instead of feeling like an outsider, criticizing leadership, you are electrified with doubt, exhilaration, and responsibility. 'What if this doesn't work?' you ask yourself everyday. Your motivational factor doubles.

"You gain a different perspective when people finally listen to you and say, 'Okay, you do have the experience. We trust you. What are we going to do now?' You turn inward and ask yourself questions you've never asked before. You realize this is somebody's dream—and it is your dream now, too—and the success of that dream falls squarely on your shoulders and the person next to you. Accepting that responsibility is harder than I thought it would be. It was much easier when it was somebody else in total control. I would always think, 'Well, if you would do it this way, you'd be successful.' Now, I was part of the problem, and part of the solution. I was totally involved. I had to think in terms of a bigger picture. Rather than being detached and judgmental, I was the one on the line. It was frightening to realize that many other people were trusting in me, listening to me, and doing what I suggested; and if I was wrong, I would hurt a lot of people. I talked to myself in my sleep, and in the shower, and all the way to work in the car. It was the biggest rush I could imagine, and I was getting it from my work! Wow! That was something I never thought would happen."

The process also changed Wardle's personal outlook. "I began to see people in a different light," she said. "Before, I was like most people in corporations who would hunker down to avoid criticism and controversy. After the process, I began to seek opinions that were different from my own. I wanted my ideas to be challenged so I could tell if they held up under fire. I take criticism differently now. I don't take it personally, but rather in an examination form. Is this information valid? If so, what action should I take to make it useful? If it isn't valid, I don't get defensive. I simply don't react to it because it has no value to me."

She continued, "It has also changed the way I deal with my family. I feel I'm more open and giving, sharing credit more and trusting more. I give trust freely now. Once you start doing that, it becomes a hard habit to break. It becomes a part of who you are. It's great to see how energized the people around you can get when they sense they are being listened to, and are trusted and valued. This process changed my outlook in a multitude of ways."

The use of large group conferencing has become a means for running the business long term. As Al Pino observed, "We use large groups to launch small groups who can deal with the detail who then report back to the large group. Course corrections are made and, subsequently, the small groups go back to modify and further explore ideas. This ebb and flow is very important to ensure involvement and continuous alignment."

"The path the company followed to achieve this alignment was not a particularly smooth one," said Pino. "There were bumps and twists and, at times, a few detours. But in the end, we arrived at a place where we could see the road ahead of us more clearly. That is what I hoped we would achieve. I find that the road to anything of real value is built in the same way. If you don't push beyond your comfort zone to the realm of chaos, you aren't really challenging yourself enough. Creativity and innovations are naturally messy, chaotic activities, but the results they yield tend to make the rocky journey well worth it."

Although they are still in the journey, Pino can see a successful resolution for everyone. "We have begun to understand and internalize the definition of real success, meaning we all succeed. For too long, our culture tended to reward people individually and encouraged competition. When the team is rewarded, people begin to appreciate the value of both individual and collective contribution."

2. GOJO: "It Ain't Done Yet!"

At GOJO, the process brought change at fundamental levels. "Perhaps the most significant insight of *The Whole Systems Approach* is the combination of process orientation and the traditional reengineering approach, with a human dynamic approach," said Joseph S. Kanfer, president and CEO. "It provides a wholly new and exciting way of viewing organizations, and the people in them."

The results of the change process on the bottom line and in the organization are clearly evident. "The process was invaluable," said COO Lerner. "The dynamics and variations of the marketplace make it hard to prove, but my judgment is that many of the tools, practices, and personal alignment changes brought into the organization during this change positioned us well to do the things we're able to do today. The important thing for leaders to understand is that this is a journey of transformation, not a project. It is the way we work now. We didn't just change, then drop the process. It is the process. We are constantly remaking ourselves. The beauty of it is we aren't done yet, and hopefully we'll never be done! This is just the first leg of the journey, but it set the course for us. That's what it did at the highest level—it set the course for us."

3. MichCon: A Long List of Tangible Benefits

MichCon, the organization operating the longest under *The Whole Systems Approach*, has been through turmoil, upheaval, confusion, and frustration. And Ewing, as CEO, has certainly had his moments of doubt. After ten years, was it worth it? "Absolutely!" Ewing answered without hesitation. "In the long term, we simply wouldn't have survived if we hadn't done it. I don't think I can underscore that point enough. I don't think any company today can compete using forms and functions that are outdated. In terms of tangible benefits, the list is long. We are a much more productive company. The operations and maintenance budget is significantly less than when the effort was launched, proof that employees are working more effectively than in the past. We've reduced our overall workforce—all through natural attrition—and increased our customer count. Our technology is superior to what it was."

In 1996, MichCon received an honorable mention for its progress in improving quality and was included as an Honor Roll member of the 1996 Michigan Quality Council's Quality Leadership Award. Their safety also improved dramatically, and they were awarded the 1997 American Gas Association Safety Award for large distribution companies in North America. Profitability is also strong, as MichCon enjoys the status of being one of the most profitable U.S. utilities. In fact, their performance for the shareholder is at the top for the industry.

"From the shareholder's perspective," observed Ewing, "we've done a splendid job. From the customer's point of view, we are performing in the top quartile, and we are moving up. From the employees' standpoint, the change has been perceived as a major opportunity. While it has been demanding and difficult for the employees and managers alike, the vast majority say their jobs are more interesting and challenging than before. I believe most of them feel as I do. This is clearly the place I want to be."

Work as Fulfillment, Purpose, and Joy

The Whole Systems Approach is a highly individual and personal one, not only for us, but for everyone who takes part in it. Total employee involvement especially acts as a crucible for all manner of change—from those involving the organizational structure and systems to the very personal.

Seeing organizations as living systems with mechanical parts lets the light through the window. Only when looking through that frame can one begin to attack the dull and diseased elements of an organization and bring them, with some confidence, to the firing lines of the future. Key to all this is the voice given to everyone in the organization—including employees, stakeholders and customers.

The idea that we could—and should—find excitement, creativity, personal growth, and deep, soul-delighting satisfaction at work is a very different legacy than the one left us by our predecessors. Certainly, it reflects a vastly different reality than the one we typically encounter in most corporate settings. We can think of nothing more soul-delighting than to help lead individuals and organizations to realize this magnificent vision. This approach provides a tremendously exciting option and opportunity for any organization to forge a new legacy for ourselves and our children. This vision has all the more clarity and power for its simplicity—we want work to be a place of joy, fulfillment, and purpose—a world of work where people and profits thrive.

The time is now to pull up the anchor, unfurl the sails, and create a legacy and a new world of work for ourselves and our organizations.

About the Authors

Cindy Adams is a principal of Maxcomm, Inc., an international organizational transformation firm. Cindy specializes in organizational transformation, cultural change, work redesign, large group conferencing, leadership coaching, teambuilding, and customer service enhancement. She holds a Master's degree in Organizational Management.

Bill Adams is a co-founder of Maxcomm, specializing in *Whole Systems Change*SM, organizational transformation and cultural change. He partners with leaders to align companies to a common purpose through a total participation strategy with all stakeholders. He holds a Master's degree in Organizational Communication. He co-authored the book *The Quest for Quality*.

Michael Bowker is a writer who has co-authored six books and more than 1,000 articles.

About Maxcomm, Inc.

Founded in 1984, Maxcomm is an international organizational change consulting and educational training firm committed to partnering with organizations to achieve outrageous business results and create "a world of work where people thrive." We focus equal attention on results and relationships, given that each are fundamental to an organization's optimum performance.

Maxcomm has developed a competency in partnering with organizations to bring about fundamental change. We respect the organizations we enter by integrating with the best of what exists, helping eliminate what is not effective, and creating what is needed. We ensure that systems are established to enable the culture to sustain and reinforce progress in the future.

Index